LIVING

A FISHERMAN'S JOURNEY

COLES
RIVER
PRESS

FAIR WINDS
—
Charley Soares

COPYRIGHT 2014 BY CHARLEY SOARES

Editing by ALL IN THE FAMILY Charles R and Karen Soares, Peter and Tina Soares.

Cover design by Andy Nebraski, Illustrations by Tom Camilleri and Zach Harvey.

Other books by Charley Soares: Stemming the Tide, Walking on Water, The Tube and Worm guide and Scratching the Surface.

Cataloging- in- publication data.
Soares, Charley L.
FISHING- striped bass, bluefish, weakfish, tautog, and fluke.
1. Sportfishing, boating, weather, fishing methods.
Title II. Atlantic coast, fish species, III Charley Soares (author)
ISBN # 978-1-63452-4179   paperback
Printed in the United States of American by Country Press

ACKNOWLEDGMENTS

First and foremost I have to thank my family. One of the things I learned early on was just how important a loving and supportive family can be. No matter what was happening in school, in sports and in my personal life my family never judged or criticized but they always offered their support and prayers. No one could ever hope to live the life I have or write a book, or in my case six other books, without the love and encouragement of someone who believed in me as my wife Lola has. She has been a steadying influence and a first class editor who has read and re-read everything I have ever written. I am also indebted to my sons Charlie and Peter and their wives, Karen and Tina who have assisted in many of these projects.

Others who have been a great help and inspiration in this and my other works are graphic artist, Andy Nebraski, talented illustrator, Tom Camilleri, and editors, Gene Borque, Kevin Blinkoff and Zach Harvey. My friends Scott Gauthier, Sue Cotta and Lee Woltman have been there when I needed them, usually on short notice. Mike and Heidi and their crew at Eagle Marine have kept me going without interruption for years providing more opportunities to be on the water catching fish, taking photos, and exploring the places that God created for fishermen.

PREFACE

What do you want to be when you grow up? How many times was this question posed to you when you were a youngster? I recall those inquiries as well as my responses and an understanding that my early exposures had a great deal to do with them. My days of wanting to be a cowboy then a soldier quickly dissolved when I was exposed to the shoreline of the Taunton River. It didn't take long for me to appreciate that this was the most fascinating place in the world, at least in the confines of my own little universe. Much of my maritime education has been well documented in my previous five books and I can only concur that without those salty old watermen and a very understanding family my life would have never been as productive or successful.

It wasn't long after I determined what I wanted to do for my life's work, realizing when I affirmed my preference to make a living as a fisherman almost everyone discouraged me from pursuing what they considered not just a pastime but a dead end vocation. From that point on I did everything necessary to establish a successful work ethic until I could make a full time living as a fishermen, author, lecturer and guide. Looking back over a long and enjoyable career I wouldn't change a thing. Perhaps the era of full time professions like my own are a thing of the past and for that reason I am most appreciative of those readers who have followed and encouraged me to provide them with stories and books they can identify with. That was the reason for this book. The old adage that a man who loves what he does never has to work a day in his life was never more accurate than when describing my own personal voyage.

ABOUT THIS BOOK

Growing up poor never prevented me from developing an appreciation for the written word, particularly everything related to fishing, hunting and the outdoors. At that time of my youth the only source of that information and entertainment was due to the benevolence of the old timers at the Weetamoe Yacht Club. Once they finished reading their magazines they would bring them to the club to share with other members. The club rule prevented any reading material from being removed from the reading room but that didn't stop my mentors from confiscating dog eared magazines destined for the pot belly to entertain and educate a boy hungry for the outdoor life. I soaked up every word from those well worn pages along with a world of enjoyment that took me from the confines of my urban working class surroundings to exotic places most of which I still only know in my dreams. During that time I learned a great deal about fishing and hunting which I later went on to put into practice.

Living The Dream is an anthology of some of my favorite articles along with unpublished works that have never, to the best of my knowledge, been presented in book form. This is not a revision of any of my previous books it is all original book material. The vast majority of my readers have expressed their preference for stories that entertain as well and inform and I have endeavored to adhere to that theme throughout this book. Fishing is a healthy form of enjoyment and relaxation that presents numerous and exciting challenges that we can all benefit from. I've enjoyed putting this book together and it is my sincere wish that you enjoy reading it.

Lleyton Charles with a striper just two pounds shy of the 30 pound goal he set for himself that beautiful July afternoon in 2014. One of the highlights of my life is being blessed with grandchildren. I have a grandson who loves to fish with his Papa and a California granddaughter who loves the water, the coast and its creatures as much as I did when I was turning over rocks along the shores of the Taunton River.

TABLE OF CONTENTS

STICKS AND STONES

WHAT PRICE WOULD YOU PAY TO FURTHER YOUR EDUCATION

Stones rained harmlessly down the banking, a few clanging loudly off the off the rusted girders of the old green bridge. The old codger may have been a renowned fisherman but he had a lousy arm. I couldn't hear his tirade over the noise of the tires whirring on the steel mesh of the draw bridge span but I could certainly read his lips. I can't tell you what he said but it didn't have anything to do with his asking for my address so he could send me a Christmas card. My scouting was worth all the trouble because on this occasion I was able to get a better, although distant view of his terminal tackle. The old timer, like many of the crusty bachelor greybeards of the day, considered kids a nuisance and many would never allow us to get within stone throwing distance of their respective lairs. At the time I reasoned that it was about keeping a guarded fishing methodology or location secret or perhaps responding to how others had treated them. The fact of the matter was that cantankerous old goat with the weak throwing arm consistently caught the most and biggest tautog I had ever seen come out of that rocky hole at the west end of the old green drawbridge

On the rare days when I beat him to this spot I caught a few small puppy tog before he arrived and began his intimidation ritual, "You had better get moving if you know what's good for you." If I dared to tarry, which I risked on occasion because of the oldsters slow and careful descent down the steep banking, down came the rocks which there was no shortage of along that stretch of shoreline. My nemesis used a tall split bamboo rod with guides affixed to both sides. An old Ocean City knuckle buster reel filled with soiled linen line was attached to that meat stick with a pair of recycled hose clamps. Unlike most fishermen of the day that employed the standard high low two hook rig this elder used a single black hand snelled hook weighted with just enough lead weight to tend bottom. On a morning when I ventured out early and took up a covert position on the utility pipes that ran under the bridge I was privy to his methodology. The pipes were at least 25-feet above the old gaffers perch and although he was constantly glancing over his shoulder to see who might be invading his space he never once looked up. After months of foiled attempts I was

1

finally able to observe the method he used to hook the fabled "White Chinners". He selected a live green crab, removed the claws then cracked the hard shell to allow the juices to escape attracting the fish to his bait. He carefully inserted the big sharp hook through the softer underbelly and out one of the smaller claws he removed permitting the razor-sharp barb to protrude just outside the shell.

When he was satisfied his bait was hooked correctly he carefully flipped his offering on the down tide side of a large slab of granite that set up a rip on the outgoing tide. Fishing a taut line he never took his thumb or left finger off his line and when a fish bit I was surprised that he did not rear back and strike as we perch fishing novices always did. He lowered the rod tip to allow slack line as the fish took the crab further into its mouth before he lifted the rod tip smartly setting the barb into the thick flesh of old leatherlips. On that morning I went to school on that cautious old man and from that day forward, imitating his tactics, my tautog scores improved dramatically. Back when I began fishing there were no mentors and very few older gents who were tolerant enough to take a kid under their wing. If your father or a kindly relative was a fisherman you were fortunate, if not, you were on your own. I have been blessed with a pretty fair memory and cannot recall much in the way of caring and nurturing between old timers and kids at least not along that sector of shoreline I called my home waters. My education came about through a series of frustrating trials and errors but those are lessons that serve me well to this very day. Learning to pay attention and knowing what to look for is as important today as it was fifty years ago. I began to understand that fishing was much more about gaining experience and attention to detail as well as giving in to my curious nature. Much more important than knowing that something is working was understanding why it worked. There were no videos or cable television shows to entertain and instruct hopeful fishermen. The closest I came to outdoor instruction and entertainment was scouring the pages of dog eared periodicals such as Field and Stream, Sports Afield and Outdoor Life that members of the Weetamoe Yacht Club discarded. Many a night my American history or geography textbooks had a copy of those magazines secreted in their folds.

Taking a distant fishing trip back then was completely out of the question so the vehicle for my travels were the photos and descriptions of the writers who had been there and accurately shared their

2

experiences. In almost every story there was information and tips on tactics and strategy particularly because I was determined to read between the lines. Those books read and re-read allowed me to accumulate a vast store of knowledge and positive techniques. While you might see two people fishing side by side in what appears to be an identical approach I am able to observe slight or significant variations. There are always differences, however, subtle and that is why one fisherman is more successful than the next. By comparison I was able to detect the slightest nuance in bait presentation, terminal tackle and other techniques that was demonstrated in their individual success ratio. Luck certainly plays some small part in the overall equation but the anglers who consistently find and catch fish do so because of their time on the water and accumulated experience. For the record I'd rather be good than lucky. Today I own a collection of over 500 books on fishing, hunting, the outdoors and natural history which contain a wealth of information which I have applied over a lifetime of outdoor pursuits, but they won't do anyone any good unless that theory is put into practice. If you are really serious about becoming a master angler you have to develop your skills and never ignore your natural curiosity. Little did I know what was in store for me when I peered down at the secretive angler? Is that trickery something I would recommend undertaking today? Hell no! With all the material available in the information era there is no reason to skulk and hide to obtain a glimpse at success. Looking back I am not proud of what I did but at the time there were no viable alternatives. That old timer has long since put down his rocks and gone on to his just rewards, however I should expound on what may have seemed like a general characterization of the fishermen of that day. It was never my intention to portray all the men of that era as rogues, in fact I eventually came to know and associate with some pretty fair and interesting old gents over these many years but I made it a point never to test their skill and accuracy at tossing rocks.

A LOOK AT SOME OF THE TACKLE IN USE WHEN THE AUTHOR WAS A BOY. CHARLEY BEGAN FISHING WITH A HANDLINE THAT CONSISTED OF A ROUND DOWEL WITH TARRED LINE WOUND AROUND IT. THE LINE WAS PULLED OFF, COILED ON THE GROUND THEN SWUNG OVERHEAD BEFORE RELEASING IT.

CITY LIGHTS

TRESPASSING AND AVOIDING THE LONG ARM OF THE LAW

The blinding shaft of light moved hurriedly and erratically across the granite slabs shining across my fingers clinging to the edge of the seawall. I held my breath as the shiny black boots walked within inches of my hide. I didn't know what caused him to be there but the patrolman was certainly unhappy about his current assignment. "Who the hell called this in? There's nobody here, dam it." The officer went on to explain to the workman that he had a busy day with two fires and a hit and run and he had just sat down to a late supper at Al Mac's Diner when the call came in. "Who the hell cares if someone was fishing off the sea wall-I don't give a damn just don't call me again." With that he stormed back up Hathaway Street and turned onto Main and back toward the glistening chrome diner that was the walking patrolman's favorite eatery in those days. God hath no fury like a beat cop whose dinner was interrupted by a nuisance neighborhood kid.

During a rather unrestrained adolescence I'd managed to avoid brushes with the law however that incident was one of many close calls. During one of my evening forays along the shoreline I had spied one of the high line fishermen catching stripers from the granite slabs that were once a docking area for boats transporting material to this area. The granite pier was built like a fortress but the pilings that protected the boats were in a state of decay. For the past few weeks I'd been working on the night watchman at the Hathaway Street power substation and began to run an errand or two for him to get in his good graces. My objective was not to steal any electrical current; it was for permission to fish the area surrounding the power plant wall without being chased out by the workforce or the day and night watchman. Just across the waterway along the Somerset shore of the Taunton River there was much better looking striper habitat but it was a much longer walk and the boats trolling there made it difficult to fish without provoking bad feelings. After sunset the fish moved in closer and spread out along the shoreline while in the grunge of the city the lights from the power station attracted the baitfish which in turn lured the stripers that preyed on them. The problem was the plant was posted and surrounded by a tall chain link fence with a string of barbed wire along the upper perimeter.

The old timer who had been fishing there was a friend of that watchman and on one occasion I observed him fillet a striper and hand it to the watchman who opened the gate for him on his way out. There was a long granite pier to the south of the power station where we took a few small bass but without any lights to attract bait it was hit or miss with a lot more missing than hitting. On the Hathaway side of the station along the chain link there was a narrow opening at a bent pipe where a car had backed into it; it wasn't very wide but big enough for skinny kid to push his way through. After a few more visits to that pier to watch the high liner catching fish I decided to take a chance and sneak in after he left. The problem was he usually quit when the good fishing was over but I figured it was worth a shot if I could get an inside look and perhaps catch a fish or two. On the night of my incursion the old fishermen was nowhere to be found and in my numerous forays I noticed that the watchman seldom if ever made rounds in the back of the building where the fishing took place. Emboldened with these particulars I pushed my rod in ahead of me and scraped my way through the breach in the fence. I maintained a low profile while walking the edge of the granite but after a half hour of casting and walking the bucktail jig along the pilings I didn't even get a sniff. I did see one very large eel chasing silversides between the pilings and could not believe how fast a serpent that large could move. It was when I was standing upright watching the eel that I heard the shout. "Hey what are you doing there"? I didn't even turn around. I ran for the fence on the side of the old Triton Boat Yard operated by Jackie Howard but could not get out so I tossed my rod over the fence and climbed down onto a rotting piling and hung on by my fingernails.

I was fortunate the watchman had not given chase but decided to run back inside to call the police. I must have been hanging on my precarious perch for almost a half hour when the beat cop showed up with his light and began cursing about the interruption of his late dinner. By the time the cop left and the watchman closed the back door my hands were numb but I managed to pull myself back up praying the rotten stump I was standing on would not give way. I crawled on my hands and knees to the tear in the fence and pushed my way through. When I reached the corner at Davol Street I looked both ways then casually walked past the front of the power station to the grassy apron where I had tossed my rod. That place may have been a striper magnet but thus far the price of admission was not worth the dangers associated with fishing there. I gave the power station a wide berth but always looked toward it with an envious glance whenever I walked by. From the time I was a young and inquisitive boy I was aware that the vast majority of fishermen flocked to the more rustic Somerset shore while two of the most secretive and successful fishermen I knew fished the grimy piers along the city's water front where they made some impressive catches of big stripers. Several years later one of the greybeards told us he had a friend who had become the new power station night watchman. After a formal introduction a few weeks later and our assurance that if we ever were caught on the property we would confess to trespassing and never divulge that the watchman was complicit in our transgressions.

We had some great trips at the power station and all along that section of the Fall River shore from the Coca Cola plant to the bottom of Ferry Street. For the record no one is more appreciative of spectacular surroundings than me and that's why I've spent most of my life fishing the waters from Westport Harbor to Jamestown Rhode Island. The truth is that from the very early on I realized that the best of the old time fishermen caught many more stripers, eels and tautog from the Fall River shore than across the river in Somerset. The reason is the structure along the city shore line provides more concentrated habitat and forage which attracts the predators. The urban glow and the city lights also play a major role. It's been rewarding fishing the aforementioned ocean waters but during my travels up and down the east coast I've fished many different locations and the best of them have been in urban areas such as the illuminated bridges from New Jersey to Florida. If you want to become more successful think about changing tactics and try fishing at night under the city lights but whatever you do don't get between a lawman and his dinner. It could get ugly.

UNCONVENTIONAL WISDOM

THE LONG DISTANCE HANDLINER

No one crowded Harold! Not unless they entertained a secret death wish. Even when his wet burlap sack was bulging with fish few men dared to invade his space. The old timer fished exclusively from shore and his favorite place was the rocky beach between two aging breakwaters that was once a Taunton River ferry landing between the Fall River and Somerset MA shorelines. As was the norm for the day he plied his sport with a huge hank of tarred line affixed to a hand crafted oblong line creel. His longest distance casts were obtained using his patented Ferris wheel cast and to watch him wind up and heave that 8-ounce sinker and a hunk of squid out towards the channel was a sight to behold.

There were usually a few envious observers but this particular Pilgrim had obviously never seen Harold, but having watched him haul a muscular striper up onto the shore he couldn't resist the temptation to get close to the table rock the old timer was positioned on. Harold turned to gauge the distance before he made his next cast, this one we called the helicopter. Rather than the circular up and down Ferris wheel motion he began twirling his line side to side in an ever winding circle, however, the dude was much too interested in making his own cast to see the 8-ounces of lead speeding towards his shoulder. The weight caught him squarely on the scapula and knocked him over face first into the water. Before he could muster enough composure to utter a complaint Harold was standing over him. "You damn fool, don't you know better than to sneak up on a man's space when he's fishing? Get your ass out of here or the next one is going to take your hat off." The thunderous voice and the imposing figure of Harold had a great deal to do with the interloper's transition from pain to fear for his life as he gathered up his gear and scurried up the banking. I'd observed the helicopter cast often enough to associate it with danger and no one, including this young daredevil, dared to stand behind Harold when he was slinging lead from the beach. That imposing figure of a man could send a lead weight and its cargo of twin hooks and a brace green crabs sailing off into the mussel bed at the edge of the channel, a feat that even the well heeled angler employing the modern spinning tackle could not come close to duplicating.

8

Depending on his objective Harold would coil his tarred line at his feet and twirl the bitter end until he gained just the right momentum. When it required a distance cast he used the helicopter method or if precise accuracy was necessary he wound up a Ferris wheel. That was the first time I watched a pilgrim move in for a peek at what was causing Harold's wet burlap sack to rumble. Anyone invading his space risked being rewarded with a purple knot from the clout of the eight ounce sinker and not just a few of them were snared with a needle sharp 6/0 Kirby buried into flesh. In those days a walk through the neighborhood would reveal those men who had adopted the more contemporary linen lines over the rough tarred hemp as many of them washed their line in a bucket then dried it on the clothes line poles somewhere between their socks and the jockey shorts. All around him Harold was being challenged. Not overtly, because few men would dare to antagonize the man with that massive muscular physique, but by the distance the new lines provided the competition when spooled on the modern rotating spool conventional reels of that era. There were a few well-heeled fishermen who were experimenting with the imported French spinning reels but they could never send a cargo of sinker and bait out to the edges of the structure.

My handlines, which I still have a few of to this day, were belatedly followed by a cranky Ocean City and well worn Pflueger. That was during the time that Penn, Ocean City and Pflueger were making converts to their rotating spool reels as they replaced the heavy knuckle busting gear that was available at the time. Harold was stubborn but he wasn't stupid. He finally caved in after developing a yen for a reel, even though it didn't provide much of an advantage over his previous technique. He reluctantly admitted that it was much neater to gather all of his line into a compact spool than have it coiled in the rocks and weed under his feet. Despite his normally intractable ways progress was making headway. Harold grudgingly moved from that handline to an ancient knuckle buster reel with a leather thumb stall attached to a crooked nine foot bamboo pole (it was by no means a rod) with used automotive hose clamps. My burly friend suffered through a frustrating season before coming to his senses. He was a frugal man who poured his sinkers into a serving spoon mold but he realized it was time to dig deep into the blueberry money his comrades accused him of having stashed away. That was when he acquired a super smooth Penn Long Beach attached to a double wrapped octagon rod with sliding ring reel seat. Although he became quite adept and returned to his former status he couldn't resist offering complaints about having to clean his reel and wash his linen line after each outing, a process that was unnecessary with his handlines. It was overkill to be so obsessive about the maintenance of his recent acquisition but the caretaker suggested that Harold derived a modicum of satisfaction from his grousing. The mainstream of my mentors reluctantly made the transition from handlines to conventional reels however the mere notion of switching over to the fixed spool of foreign spinning reels was not just unthinkable it was considered downright un-American. Even the few who admitted being prepared to make that move were restrained by peer pressure.

Not long after the first American made spinning reels hit the market the old conventional standby was relegated to second class status. While spinning provided a significant advantage for fishermen interested in casting and working lures or jigs at distance, the bait fishermen welcomed the arrival of advanced conventional casting reels like the Penn Squidder and the Jigmaster. Over the last several decades the vast majority of anglers came of age in a spin fishing oriented environment with little or no background and experience with the conventional method. From the time I purchased my first Penn Squidder on credit I have been an advocate of the rotating spool reels because of what they provide in the way of power and control. Discounting the stiff solid glass rods and thick heavy lines of the past my existing tackle allows me to cast eels and big plugs and fish all forms of outsized live baits

Aboard my boat many a died- in- the- oilers technique spin fishermen overcame their inhibitions and were converted to conventional tackle. They soon discovered that even if their medium heavy spinning gear was capable of placing a big live eel in gnarly bass habitat it was often not up to the task of pulling the fish that lived there away from the protection of it. Today's state of the art standup spinning outfits with the brawny rods they beat tuna with are not what you want to spend a day casting to stripers with. A man whose name you would immediately recognize came aboard one day and noticed that Charlie Cinto and I were using heavy conventional tackle with three backup outfits of the same class in the rod holders. He sported a very expensive spinning outfit that could loft big eels a fair distance, but two of the bass he hooked over a certain boulder field took him into the stones and shredded his leaders. He managed a 28-pound fish but his experience told him that he had lost two fish of a much higher class because he could not put the brakes on them or turn them around. On that day we accounted for bass of 45, 41 and 38-pounds and we estimated the two fish he lost were in that same weight class. Although he politely declined my offer of a conventional outfit the next time he came aboard he was armed with a Penn Torque reel spooled with 65-pound braid and a live bait rod from the same custom designer who builds my gear.

In previous articles I have alluded to heavy meat sticks, but for the record I do not employ any such tackle. After decades of testing and experimenting in the habitat where I have found broomtail bass my gear consists of a Penn Torque TRQ 15 and a Penn 535 High Speed spooled with 65 test Power Pro or Tuff Line on seven foot medium fast blanks. We still fish the two for five spot and occasionally we get lucky and pull three rather than two fish of the five hooked bass, but some days all five stripers make it to safety. As I've said before some bass that habituate these difficult environments are just not meant to be captured.

OLD HABITS DIE HARD

Back in the day when jumbo bass were known as "bulls" and the Latin name for stripers was "Roccus", life was good and fishing was even better. A keeper striper was any fish over 16-inches and at that time very few of the fish we caught were much smaller than 18-inches. Drapes Fish market was paying me an average of 25 cents per pound at a time when thirty cents would buy a chow mein sandwich and a coke at most of the area Chinese restaurants. It was a great time to be alive. My neighbors Albert and Ray were unemployed laborers who resorted to digging clams and worms along the Taunton River shoreline then fishing for tautog, perch and the occasional striper that moved in close enough to snatch one of their sharp Kirby hooks. The old timers were sitting on the back porch of the Weetamoe Yacht Club smoking pipes and building their blade and bead spinner rigs to troll worms for stripers and I was perhaps the only 12-year old boy from the neighborhood gainfully employed running errands to the Bridge Diner for pocket change and "chartering" for cash by rowing a few of the old timer's boats while they trolled for bass. It was the mid 1950's and despite difficult economic times no one was sleeping in cardboard boxes or alleyways or sitting on street corners with their hat in hand pleading for a hand out. If someone was down and out their family would lend a hand and if there weren't any family connections there was always the benevolence of a neighbor or a compassionate religious congregation. Dad was quick to remind me the only helping hand I ever needed was the one at the end of my arm and he advocated that any man who could dig a hole would never be hungry or out of work. Good advice back then and right on the mark today.

I know now that being born and living alongside the river probably saved my life and provided me with the values that have steered me along the sometimes precarious straight and narrow. We took as much as the rivers and bays would allow and sometimes more than we needed but nothing ever went to waste. I can recall returning home from fishing with every intention of selling my catch but occasionally Mom had other plans. As the recipient of good works from our family, friends and neighbors she preached the gospel of sharing so she would instruct me as to how to distribute my catch. Fillets went to the woman who lost her husband or the man who was injured and out of work or the lady with four children whose husband left town with the bar maid. I never kept an accounting of those contributions but in the long run I'm certain that I came out at the top of the ledger and way ahead of anything I ever donated in good faith. Although fishing was allowed for any species all year round with few if any restrictions it was usually Good Friday that became the unofficial start of the season with winter flounder on the menu. Perhaps my recollections of conditions on those openers were influenced by the good nuns at St. Michael's school who discoursed on the consequences of the crucifixion and the rendering of the sanctuary curtain during that terrible storm. With those solemn events in mind my memories of Good Fridays fishing weather were seldom of warm and sunny spring days. The fact that most of the residents in the predominately Catholic north end where I lived had Good Friday off was not lost on this fisherman. Back then when winter flounder was an abundant species they were one of the most popular and sought after fish. We could toss a handline baited with a freshly dug seaworm off the Brightman Street or Slades Ferry Bridge, the Naval Reserve Pier or the entire shoreline of the Taunton River with the reasonable expectation of catching enough flounder for a fresh seafood meal.

The prime winter flounder fishing didn't get underway until at least mid April and ran well into late May before these bottom huggers had completed their annual spawning ritual and moved out to deeper water. I don't ever recall topping off a galvanized pail with flounder on the eve of the Easter celebration yet I can't ever remember having to purchase fish of any kind for our Good Friday meal. Long before I was old enough to catch fish on my own someone would donate flounder or if we were lucky one of the neighbors would take a day off and make a trip on a party boat then share prime fillets of cod and pollock. Today flounder fishing is nothing more than a fond memory and the once reliable tautog fishery, which kicks off on the bloom of the dandelions, has also fallen on hard times. I can't ever recall any restrictions on the inshore cod fishery which any man who owned a trailerable boat could take advantage of. One of the greybeards I mated for had a makeshift trailer built from the rear axle of a retired pickup truck. When the winter weather provided a window we travelled to Plymouth where it seemed that the cod were always just outside the harbor with their mouths wide open. There were times during the week when I was in school that he and two other gents filled that flat bottom skiff to the gunwales with cod and pollock and the occasional yellowtail flounder that opened its maw wide enough to swallow the firm conch baits or the fresh quahogs they used. That was an era I wish my younger readers could have witnessed.

When I was a boy there were no local ponds within walking distance of my home so we never developed a taste for sweetwater fishing until much later on. Sometime in my very early childhood my uncle Vinnie, a non fisherman, took me fishing along the banks of the South Watuppa pond and from that first moment when the bobber disappeared beneath the surface I was hooked for life. My first freshwater fish was a bluegill and our mixed bag for that first trip included yellow perch and tiny smallmouth bass. I didn't get back to that pond again for many years but I was smitten with the fast and furious action of worm dunking in fresh water. During the winter most of us are just looking or thinking of something to put a bend in a rod but the options in saltwater are limited to cod, pollock and haddock; species which most of us are not quite ready to pursue unless we take advantage of the party boats that sail out of nearby harbors. What we really need is a healthy species close to home to pull the string. This is the time of the year when I lament the passing of those fantastic white perch runs in the Palmer, Assonet, Weweantic and Wareham Rivers. The perch was a species that arrived in late January or early February and provided consistent action until late May. White perch are aggressive fish, hit like their striper cousins, and are one of the best tasting of all saltwater panfish. Those silver gamesters have begun staging a modest return in a few of the aforementioned rivers and on a chilly spring morning last year we made our first significant catch, one that necessitated my setting up the fillet table for what later became a much appreciated feast of golden fried fillets

Hope springs eternal and while I do not have visions of the return of that 1950's fishery I invite you to join me in the hunt for these emerging schools of silver fish that can bring a smile and glimmer of hope to a winter weary angler. Change is inevitable and I have reluctantly accepted most of it but I do have some advice for the so-called scientist who was responsible for changing the striper's name from Roccus to Morone. Mind your own damn business!

FAT OF THE LAND

FEEDING THE FAMILY DURING LEAN TIMES

The overpowering scent of vinegar burned my nostrils yet this visit to the basement processing operation was well worth the discomfort. Over the years I had enjoyed the pickled onions and mild sweet peppers that were being preserved in this damp room with rugged fieldstone walls and sheets of plywood covering the dirt floor. Some might envision that food for human consumption being prepared in the cellar of a three tenement house might be lacking in the sanitation front however that was never the case. The onions and peppers were home grown in the garden on the side of the hill overlooking the Taunton River on a small patch of land our family friend leased from the railroad for the princely sum of $ 1.00 a year. During the hour I was visiting with the self made farmer I watched his wife make three trips down to the basement with a huge steaming pot covered with a white towel under which were boiled and sterile Mason jars to be used to store the pungent mixture. Long before laws mandated the enhancement of food handling and the use of latex gloves this canner was using boiling hot water to wash his hands between each of the several processes. He carefully poured a cup of his secret pickling mixture into a long row of sanitized jars then using long wooden tongs filled the glass containers with miniature onions and a combination of red and yellow sweet peppers before adding a small red hot pepper which added a little bite to the brew.

Our family friend wasn't going through this procedure just to save money because at the time you could purchase a jar of pickled peppers for small change. He and his wife were famous for their secret blend of spices, and vinegar that distilled into the best onions and peppers I had ever tasted. The mill hand who transitioned into an afternoon farmer did not sell his delicious products but he did barter them. He loved fish and we loved pickled peppers and onions. He walked from his tedious job in the textile mill to a much more physical duty on his land where these labors of love put a smile on his face. During the summer while he was hoeing between rows of vegetables I would walk by on my way to the water to hunt blueshell crabs or fish for white perch. On most days I would return before dusk while he was just putting away his tools and preparing to lock up his fenced in garden. Yes, even at that time there was always the danger that his crops might disappear if left unprotected but the black and white mongrel that wagged its tail and licked my face when I visited would launch itself against the wire barrier with teeth barred if I got too close to the gate when the owner was absent.

Every day of his adult life this man carried a black lunch box with a thermos of hot soup tucked up inside the cover when he left his home at 5:30 AM to walk to the old Sagamore Mills in order to arrive early for his 6:00 AM to 2:00 PM shift as a weaver in the huge granite mill building. As with many of the gents of his day Manuel smoked a pipe and blended his own pipe tobacco and the only time I can recall seeing his mouth devoid of that chewed up stem was when he was preparing food. He usually went directly from the mill to his little piece of heaven and unlocked the gate to the greeting of his ecstatic dog. Unless it was storming, our friend was known to pray for rain and every evening he and his devoted wife would walk to that little patch of green, their oasis in this urban district on the little piece of heaven on the hillside. Here they enjoyed a panoramic view of the river and all the maritime activity along the perimeter of this background that consisted of rows of six decker tenement houses most built within hand shaking distance to their next door neighbors. The good woman would usually be seen clothed in her floral house dress and apron and carrying their warm supper and a jug of tap water or home brewed wine.

I often visited with them while they ate their dinner and thought of how lucky they were to have this retreat away from work and the monotony of household chores where they actually worked harder tilling and tending the soil than they did at their respective employment. As we stared across the river to the Somerset shore they talked of their plans to buy a piece of land in the "country" which was what we called that green belt on the west side of the Taunton River. My dad was fond of saying if you didn't have a dream, a realistic vision for your future you might just as well roll over and give up. Dreams are what inspire and keep life interesting and challenging and even though you might never fully attain your objective those aspirations kept us in a positive frame of mind. I can picture myself walking up the hill from Patty Connors boat rental shack with a bucket of blueshell crabs or a mess of white perch to share with our friends. They would be sitting on the bench he crafted out of driftwood planks eating home cooked food and **Living Their Dream**. The man in the bibbed blue farmers jeans covered with cotton thread came to life when he stepped through that gate. I never left that garden without a piece of homemade bread slathered in butter, a head of lettuce or a paper bag of pole beans, squash or tomatoes for mom's kitchen.

Although they never offered their peppers for sale I watched him pocket a few dollars from time to time as neighbors came calling for his famous produce. I once was witness to a friendly argument with a neighbor who came to buy two jars for which our friend would take no money. The man left then closed the door behind him when we heard a scratching and watched a small manila pay envelope slide under the door sill. Manuel smiled and said that happens all the time. The gardener was never idle and in the late fall into winter he sold a bit of moonshine and flavored brandy made from grapes grown on his own vines. His liquor still looked like something out of a plumber's nightmare with burner, coiled copper tubing ending with a tiny tube where the finished product dripped into the big glass container. In its original form that liquid was capable of paralyzing the vocal chords of most whiskey drinkers but when he began diluting and flavoring it that brew became a favorite holiday libation. When dad was alive he and Manuel would occasionally share a cold beer and although my mom never imbibed we always had a bottle of his flavored brandy in the cupboard for medicinal needs. Whenever I came down with a heavy cold or fever mom would heat the brandy add some sugar and coax me to drink it before bedtime. I slept like a drunken sailor, sweat like a marathon runner and usually awoke the next morning much better because of mom's cocktail. Back in the day when we didn't have money, which was quite often, we bartered and traded goods and services.

If you have been paying attention you may have noticed that we are suffering through a difficult financial period and if you consider that an understatement you are absolutely correct. We have all had to tighten our belts and make adjustments to get by but helping less fortunate neighbors and friends should not take a backseat in these troubled financial times. Back in the days when Manuel worked in the mill he confessed that paying a mortgage and living on his single income would have been impossible without his knack for the trading and bartering that he required to keep his head above water. Today it is not as easy to live off the fat of the land because the land has become so lean. So many things have changed since those days on the little garden plot on the riverbank but the desire to survive is still alive and well. Over the years I have faced some challenges and I have found that if I was willing to work hard at whatever employment was available I could provide for my family and keep my head above water. One winter during difficult financial times I dug clams almost daily and sold them to a few local taverns. I dug post holes in frozen ground and hauled shingles up a 30 foot ladder to a steep roof then went off to a friend's wood lot and cut fuel for the wood stove. I once baited hooks on a commercial tub trawler for a ride to the winter cod grounds where I jigged for cod between sets. Those white belly cod the skipper allowed me to keep put quality food on our table and on good trips I sold the rest for cash. Despite the fact that we live in modern times the desire to become more self sufficient continues to burn brightly in the DNA of many of the fishermen I am proud to call my friends.

THERE ONCE WAS A TIME WHEN IT WAS POSSIBLE TO LIVE OFF THE FAT OF THE LAND, BUT THAT IS NOT THE CASE TODAY. A COUPLE THAT FARMED THEIR LAND, CAUGHT THEIR OWN FISH, AND BARTERED FOR NECESSITIES CAME AS CLOSE TO LIVING THAT DREAM AS ANYONE THE AUTHOR KNEW.

KNIFES FOR KIDS

THE WAY IT WAS THE WAY IT SHOULD BE

The nattily dressed woman was so flustered her anxiety prevented her from verbally communicating the warning that was constrained within her throat. After her animated pointing and gyrations she was finally able to blurt out a few words. "Can't you see that child" she gasped? "He has a knife." I assured her I could not only see the boy but I was the one who had given him the knife. The "child" (a competent lad of ten years) was skinning fish on the cutting board of my boat as weekend tourists walked along the docks at Sakonnet Point on a warm summer afternoon. My friend's son was helping me prepare our catch to take back to our family and friends and the boy was actually a big help. Two years ago on a trip with his father he asked if I'd show him how to clean our catch. With his father's permission I took the time to demonstrate how to skin fillets, a task he took to with enthusiasm.

It had been his second trip aboard my boat and he was bursting with enthusiasm and questions, so many that his father cautioned him to be quiet. I reminded his dad about how inquisitive we were as boys watching the old timers fish, clam and clean their catches at a time when children were not only expected to be seen and not heard but as far as some of those old curmudgeons were concerned it was better if we weren't there at all. Thanks to our experiences as boys filled with expectation and thirsting for knowledge we treat children the way we wished we had been dealt with as youngsters. I took the time to show the boy how to wear a modern fillet glove which protects against nicks and cuts and to handle the fish away from him in such a manner as to make the skinning a safe uncomplicated task.

The youngster took to the chore like a duck to water anxious to show us he was disposed to do his part as compensation for the fishing trips we took him on. The woman could not believe that a grown man would allow a boy to handle an eight-inch knife because it was such a dangerous tool. What she didn't know was akin to the bumper sticker you might see affixed to a teacher's car, the one that states that "if you think education is expensive-try ignorance." If a child without the awareness as to the potential harm a knife could do in the hands of an inexperienced person were taught to either use it properly or educated

20

in the damage these sharp tools are capable of there would be less accidents with knives and other cutting implements. The youngster with the knife that the aforementioned woman was so disturbed about was not only using a knife but that filleting tool belonged to him. Also, with the permission of his parents, I had made a Christmas gift of that knife to him once he demonstrated how capable and responsible he was. After he was through with his cutting duties I ran it through the sharpener to hone the edge before he washed the knife and coated it with mineral oil. The knife remained in the locker on my boat and no one else was allowed to use that tool except for the boy who took great pride in showing off his skills to people, many who weren't capable of cleaning their own catch.

There was a time, not very long ago, when almost every man I knew from mill workers to bank presidents carried some form of pocket knife. They were used for whittling, cutting line, twine and rope, opening letters, trimming fingernails and numerous other tasks that knifes were designed to perform. Several years ago I wrote about the Christmas Case, the knife I purchased from Benny's Hardware store in the village section of the north end of Fall River. I was about 13 years old at the time and didn't have two nickels to rub together yet Benny had faith in me and my potential as an outdoorsman and he sold me that handsome Case knife on credit. I had been using knives since the age of seven or eight when my dad allowed me to open and close the gentlemen's knife he carried in his suit pants pocket.

Looking back at Dad's knife, it was tiny compared to the one the boy was using to skin the fish, but it had two blades, a scissors and a nail file and screw driver. What more could a shoe salesman want when it came to utility? Dad showed me how to hand off and accept a knife from another person - always with the knife closed and if it was open and working, you passed it by the bottom of the handle with the blade pointing away from both parties. Several years later an old timer gave me his worn Barlow knife and although thousands of passes over the hand stone had robbed the blade of most of its heft it was still very sharp and made a good whittling tool - just right for any tackle box, fishing or camping situation. Today the same knife that was considered an indispensable tool is now considered a dangerous weapon. The knives have not changed, at least not very much, but people and their perceptions have. In this politically correct age of dangerous notions everything is considered a weapon rather than a tool. My grandson was eight years old when I gave him a Gerber utility pliers similar to the one his father wore when he mated on our boat at about the same age. He is well aware that the Gerber is a tool and not a weapon and he has put that tool to good use removing hooks from scup and fluke. He does not take the Gerber home as it stays here in Swansea ready for him to wear when he steps aboard our boat or follows us into the field.

I don't understand why people can't comprehend that proper training in anything is so important and that ignorance is the existent danger. Eddie Eagle is a safety mascot of the NRA that teaches school children what to do when they come across a firearm in the home or on the street. The lesson is simple; educate your children to prepare them for future encounters with anything that might hurt them or others around them.   This includes knives, firearms, as well as electrical and battery powered tools that may be left around the house when effecting repairs.

Christmas has always been so very special to our family and more so lately because of the early experiences during difficult financial times when I knew I didn't get what I wished for but I was so very thankful for what little I received. Some of you may remember the Boy Scout displays in many department and specialty stores. Every Christmas during my early years I would walk around that exhibit looking at the Boy Scout knives and wishing I could afford one. Yet despite those desires and high hopes of earning enough money to purchase one, my longing never came to realization. Over the years I've come across several of those knives at sporting shows, swap meets and antique shows and I've made up for those yearnings. My bride claims that I buy every Boy Scout knife I see but that is certainly not the case, I just buy the nice ones. Today a modest collection of Boy and Girl Scout knives adorns the shelves one of my glass curio cabinets waiting to be passed on to well behaved boys and girls who are deserving of a collectable that eluded me during my formative years. It has always been my wish that my fellow fishermen would take a page from an old book and teach their children skills that will come in handy and protect them at some time in the future.

What were once considered the tools of the trade are now considered lethal weapons. It's sad to see what has become of our society. Knives are important tools aboard a boat and the author has knives positioned at several locations around his boat to bleed fish, to cut lines or whatever else a sharp tool is needed.

BENEATH THE SURFACE

What would you give for a glance at the bottom?

As a kid I was given to fanciful day dreaming and pondering on what I now know were improbable situations. While sitting on the granite base of the second bridge pier I would close my eyes and contemplate what was taking place beneath the surface of the calm water. I wondered what it would be like to drain all the water from that portion of the river and see what creatures lived beneath the limitations of my vision. Where were the white perch that were here at this same time yesterday feeding like they hadn't eaten in weeks and what about the huge striper I saw cruising the piers at dusk hunting for a large blue shell crab or an eel for its evening meal? Were those crafty and elusive blue shell crabs holding onto the old wooden pilings deeper than my sight could penetrate and were the eels really under or around the rocks hiding from predators until darkness waiting for that time when they could leave their subterranean lairs and prey on small baitfish along the edges of the eel grass? I had so many questions and theories and so little time, or so I thought.

Today I'm considerably older and slightly more affluent than the impressive young boy who spent most of his free summer time with wet sneakers a hand line and a can of bait worms prowling the Taunton River shoreline. A bit wiser perhaps but no less prone to dreaming because I'm still very mindful of the marine life and the constant struggle of what is eating or being eaten that goes on in the depths and out of view. These days while I'm traversing over the skin of my favorite surface, my attention is divided between the water up ahead and the screen on the chart recorder which alerts me to every lump and bump as well as the presence of habitat, forage and predatory fish. When I began fishing from a boat the most modern aids I had at my disposal were an old box compass compliments of a former tug boat deck hand that spent his summers on the porch of the Weetamoe yacht club and a pocket watch with a missing crystal. The watch was the gift of a person who shall remain unnamed although I'll share the circumstances of its acquisition with you. He was a giant of a man prone to drinking too many boiler makers on a payday but not one to tolerate drunken fools who abused or bullied quiet working men or the uptown floozies who showed up ever Friday afternoon intent on fleecing men out of a portion of their hard earned wages.

On a warm Friday evening, as I was approaching one of the village cafés, I heard the unmistakable clamor of a major brawl so I stopped in my tracks two doors up from the open doorway of the bar. From the noise and howls emanating from that workingman's tavern it sounded like a free for all and just as I was about to cross the street to avoid the entrance a man crashed through the screen door then rolled off the sidewalk and into the gutter. I stopped to look when the remainder of the door flew open and the shadow of the dock worker appeared in the doorway as he held and throttled another man he was lifting off the ground. He pinned the second man up against the fender of the black Buick Road Master that was usually parked there and proceeded to read him the riot act. Dad told me there were several types of drunks some happy, some stupid and a few ugly-mean and to avoid each category at all costs. Heeding his words I headed for Potvin's Shell station only to find that my friend Ray was off that night. I proceeded to the shoreline and the yacht club where the group of codgers on the bench put me to work. They collected their change and dispatched me to McDermott's Diner for coffee and pastry.

As I was leaving the diner the dock worker was walking down the opposite side of the street stopping when he saw me with my box of provisions. He said he needed a coffee and asked if I'd run into the diner and get him one. This was a man who had always been particularly kind to me so I left him with my box and fetched him a large steaming black coffee. When I returned he refused the change from his dollar even though I told him I'd only earn a dime or so from my original errand. He smiled and ruffled my hair and that was when I looked down to see blood staining the pocket of his right pant leg. I hesitated but found the courage to bring that to his attention as he obviously had not felt or wasn't bothered by what appeared to be a nasty wound. He reached into his pocket and removed the old circular watch with a broken crystal that had apparently been shattered during the altercation. He unsnapped it from the chain, listened for the ticking and asked me if I owned a watch to which I replied in the negative. Handing me the watch he suggested I remove the remainder of the glass and visit him at his boatyard some weekday evening when he would show me how to use a watch and compass to plot time and courses. I thanked him and took the watch wrapping it in my handkerchief and ran all the way back to the club where I was chastised for taking so long on that coffee run.

Reluctant to take the dock worker up on his offer I asked the caretaker for advice and he explained how to make timed runs between buoys to determine speed and distance a lesson that has proven invaluable to this very day because if I learned anything it was that expensive electronics did not make anyone a fisherman. In all the years and all the water that has passed under my hulls I've never obtained that look beneath the surface that the boy had wished for but I have learned how to read the shoreline which is an accurate indicator of the kind and type of bottom falls away into the depths. You will seldom if ever locate and catch predatory game fish over smooth sandy bottom because these fish use structure to hide and ambush the baitfish, lobsters and crabs they feed on. Baitfish will seldom stray from the protection of rocks and weeds where they must hide unless they are driven out of that cover by the predators. If I told you I knew where just about every rock, ledge and piece of structure between Westport Harbor and Jamestown Rhode Island was located you'd probably scoff at that statement. The fact is that I have been traversing those waters for well over 50 years and if I close my eyes I can visualize that entire section of dangerous coastline because I am intimately familiar with it. Most of you can make your way in the total darkness of your home from your bedroom to the kitchen or bathroom without the aid of artificial light because of your familiarity with your surroundings you know exactly where everything is located. The same is true with the ocean where nothing ever moves except for logs, debris, lobster pots and other forms of flotsam and jetsam. Without the aid of a side scan sonar or some of the more recent offerings in bottom scanning electronics we will never be able to "pull the plug" on our oceans and rivers to see what they look like when they are not covered with that protective layer of water. Thanks to a dock worker, the deck hand, the caretaker and a great deal of time on the water I've learned that there are other ways to distinguish what lies on the bottom however that is the material and substance for a future article.

CONNIE CODNER RELEASES A KEEPER BASS IN THE NAUSET BEACH AREA OF CAPE COD. SURF FISHERMEN HAVE TO RELY ON PURE INSTINCT TO LOCATE FISH WHILE BOATING ANGLERS HAVE MODERN ELECTRONICS TO LOCATE FISH AND PRODUCTIVE STRUCTURE.

INTRODUCTION TO THE SEA TROUT

THE RETURN OF THE WEAKFISH

The two boys raced the length of the shoreline, scurrying from pier to pier excitedly quizzing every fisherman they came upon but much to their dismay they were encountering more questions than answers. One boy was proudly holding their prize, occasionally submerging the fish in the cool water to highlight its brilliant coloration while the other searched for someone who might solve their puzzle. They were not all that concerned about the fate of the fishing tackle they left unattended on the wharf after landing the most unusual specimen. The youthful fishermen were totally frustrated in their quest for information until they came upon an old gent perched atop a galvanized bucket who was in the process of topping off a burlap bag full of white perch along the east bank of the Taunton River. The man examined the fish closely, carefully opening its mouth and checking its spiked fangs while speaking to the fish as one might to a long lost friend. He held the fish up to the sun grinning broadly and stated "you've caught a "squeteague". My friend and I stared at each other none the wiser for that morsel of information. We had also been perch fishing until we caught this beautiful speckled creature which we, along with most of the shoreside residents we had come upon, could not identify. We were about to run off, when the old gent motioned for us to sit and listen.

He patiently explained that there was once many squeteague or weakfish (as they were sometimes called because of their tender mouths) many years ago before the eelgrass blight descended upon the bay. He hoped our fish was an indication that the trout were beginning to repopulate their former haunts in our bays and rivers. Our tutor reminisced about catching numerous squet in the four to seven pound range at the headwaters of the Lee and Coles River off Mt Hope Bay and the larger specimens which took up residence in the deep hole off the north face of Gould Island in the Sakonnet River where they gorged on Mantis shrimp. The experienced angler informed us that he had never set out to fish for them exclusively but they were a welcome incidental catch for him and those who fished for scup or black sea bass. The year previous to our encounter one of the old timer's friends caught a speckled sea trout on a spinner and worm rig while trolling for stripers under the Mt. Hope Bridge in lower Narragansett Bay. That 10-pound fish caused quite a stir as its captor made the rounds of the working class taverns and hardware and sporting goods stores in the village later that day. We learned a lot about fishing and near-shore history from that gentleman, particularly about the squeteague which is sometimes referred to as the sea trout, weakfish, greyfish, or tiderunner over the expanse of their range.

Most importantly we were advised never to take anything for granted. Over the many decades since that first encounter with the stately sea trout I have witnessed cycles of plenty and times of scarcity such as those we have encountered over the past several decades. By any name the squet is a favorite with any angler who appreciates them for their selectivity, fighting qualities, and as excellent table fare. When the fabled resurgence of weakfish occurred in Mt Hope Bay waters in the mid 70's, I was fortunate to be ahead of most local anglers in looking for the large roe laden sea trout which visited the structure of Brayton Point, Gardners Neck and up along the thick eel grass rich shores on the west bank of the Lee River. My timely information came from my friend Tony who operated the Fish Trap Company at Sakonnet Point Rhode Island. He informed me of the early weakfish arrivals which showed up in their lighthouse fish traps in the upper Sakonnet River. Over the many years I have known this family they were responsible for keeping me abreast of the movement of many of our migratory species. Many saltwater fishermen caught their first, and regrettably for some their only, sea trout in those days of plenty while fishing squid or soft bait for other species in the waters of the Sakonnet River, Narragansett and Mt. Hope Bay as well as up into the upper reaches of the Taunton and Assonet Rivers.

Putting that information to work I began fishing the warm water outfall of the Brayton Point Power Plant then along the west shore of the Lee River with nothing to show for three days. On the fourth day I caught two eight pound stripers trolling worms off Gardners Neck and on the third pass I caught a five pound weakfish. On the flood tide I moved from the point down to the west shore of the Lee where I began prospecting and spotted the dorsal and tail fins of a pod of weakfish grubbing for grass shrimp. I cautiously began casting a half ounce Smilin' Bill bucktail, seasoned with herring juice, above them and began working it back toward the hungry trout which jumped all over it. Although I have caught Squeteague on poppers and small surface swimmers they are usually more receptive to jigs, plastics and small tins worked slowly and close to the bottom. I kept six weaks in the five pound class that day and in the following month I introduced numerous fishermen to this esteemed visitor to our New England waters. In successive years the size of the fish matured into 10-pounds and the occasional 12-pound specimen but that size class marked the end of their incursions into Mt Hope Bay for the next twenty years. Northern weakfish are a very cyclical species which are given to radical swings of population and it seems that only when the species is on the rise that we see them venture into our waters.

In the course of the next cycle of abundance from 1995 to 2005 I put clients on some outsized specimens up to 13-pounds which are commonly referred to as Tide Runners. In keeping with their cyclic nature they suddenly vanished until 2012 when there were scattered reports of very spotty fishing in estuaries. Then in 2013 when another shot of barely legal weaks found their way up to their northern extreme a new generation of anglers was introduced to the yellow tails. With no small measure of remorse and a considerable amount of guilt I must confess that while fishing live eels off Newport and Sakonnet in the 1970's I was cursing the big weaks that picked up our live eel striper baits, piercing their heads and killing them with their sharp pointed teeth. Tiderunners do not strike with the ferocity of a striper then take off on those signature bass runs. They grab the bait by the head and usually move off slowly. At least that was our experience over the two seasons the big trout took up residence in the ocean waters. Today I'm a bit wiser and much more appreciative so I would sacrifice a dozen prime live bass eels for the opportunity to once again match wits with this prince of salt water game fish. In late May of last year I began receiving e-mails and photos of weakfish that were caught in Mattapoisett Harbor, up inside the Weweantic and in the grass flats inside of Onset Bay towards the eastern end of Buzzards Bay. Later in June I received two confirmed reports from striper fishermen using fresh squid on fish_finder rigs who landed 18-inch weakfish inside the Bristol Narrows at the entrance to the Kikimuit River in Mt Hope Bay.

Most fishermen are familiar with the natural cycles of many of our saltwater species however those of the weakfish are drastic. For that reason I would never suggest that you set out on a weakfishing expedition because more than likely you will be disappointed.

Although I have no scientific justification whatsoever for this assumption, based on my experience in this fishery I believe that 2015 could provide better sea trout fishing in our area. While the current size and bag limit of just one fish a day over a 16-inch minimum size is an indication of the uncertain circumstances of this valued species I don't believe our primitive rod and reel tactics are capable of inflicting any harm on this prized species. This spring I'm going to begin my search for weaks where I first discovered them in the tributaries of lower Narragansett and Mt Hope Bay. You might want to take a look because if you find one you won't be disappointed.

A LADY ANGLER ADMIRES THE COLORATION AND SHARP FANGS OF A NARRAGANSETT BAY WEAKFISH THAT FELL VICTIM TO A PLASTIC BAIT WORKED SLOWLY ALONG THE EEL GRASS.

CHAPTER TWO

REPUTATIONS ON THE LINE

HOOKED ON A GAMBLE

THE OCTOBER CASH RUN

The breakwater beacon faded into the early morning sea smoke as the little bass boat made the turn out of the sleepy harbor. Dousing the deck with a bucket of saltwater is not the customary way to launch a fall fishing trip, but with slippery hoar frost covering the deck it was a necessity. It was 29 degrees at 4:45 AM and the Back River was a thick cloud of sea smoke. Chilly October mornings were always a challenge for the old hand choked, single carburetor inboard, but with meticulous maintenance and a few prayers she coughed to life and warmed up to a smooth and reassuring idle. In the dangerous habitat where she earned her living there was no room for less than flawless reliability. After two days of very poor fishing and a spate of gusty northwest winds I had the ocean to myself. The conventional wisdom among the local striper men was that with few if any stripers moving through and the ocean recovering from a stomach ache it wasn't worth leaving a warm bed, so they waited for someone else to go out and invest their time and fuel before they made another effort. I had played this game before and the last thing I envisioned was being a scout for some lazy pin hookers.

There is a bit of the gambler in every fisherman I've met and some of us have been known to take that inclination to the next level. I wasn't planning on rolling the dice or sitting in on a game of seven card stud; in my situation my gamble was much more precarious. Vacation time was something many of my friends had come to expect because when they took their week or two off from their respective employment they anticipated a paycheck before they left or when they returned. Not so for the self employed. At the time I was working as a claims investigator under a Massachusetts and Rhode Island Private Investigator's license and was paid by the case but only upon conclusion which could take months and often required providing testimony before a magistrate in Workman's Compensation Claims court or a judge during civil or criminal proceedings. For that reason I could not just take one day at a time, so in order to clear my schedule I blacked out two weeks in October well in advance of that date to free up time for fishing the fall run. While I always tried to save a few bucks to have in reserve it never seemed to work that way so the pressure of trying to make enough to pay for my "vacation" weighed heavy on me. I usually had a pair of crisp $ 20's tucked away in my wallet for emergency fuel and bait but prayed I wouldn't have to dig into it before Christmas.

The general consensus was that the storm had blown all the fish through and if anything perhaps a pod or two might be moving down from the west end of the canal along the north shore of Buzzards Bay and westward to their natal rivers. According to my imperfect math I had lost two days of fishing or two days' pay, but thanks to Uncle Ernie I spent that time digging post holes and erecting a fence for one of his customers. Dad said if you knew how to dig a hole you would never be out of work. I had no idea if the vast majority of the migration had moved through Buzzards Bay or decided to move out through Vineyard Sound, but if there was a vanguard it was up to me to find out. We rode the swell over weed filled water until I turned southeast at the Islands and headed for Warren's Point. Out of the corner of my eye I caught a glimpse of terns hovering around the edge of a white water breaker and went over to investigate. I had two spinning rods, two wire line trolling rods and a conventional casting/live bait rod on board so I grabbed for the spinner with the chrome hammered Hopkins No-Equal with the single hook bucktail and sent it out into the backwash. The take was immediate and violent. The drag on the green Penn was screaming as the 20-pound Stren melted off the spool. What the hell had I hooked into? The fish moved over and out of the breaker and came to the surface tail walking and head shaking trying to spit the lure from its jagged jaws before seeking the depths where it put a strain on the tackle. By the time I stuck the hook from the long bamboo gaff into its evasive form we had drifted almost 300 yards.

Two solid blows from the heavy priest subdued the 12-pound alligator enough to allow me to extract the hook, now minus the bucktail, and slip it into the fish box. Several more casts along the reef went unrewarded so I racked the rod and headed for Warrens Point. The hump from the leftover swell restricted my inside pass so I headed for deeper water and paid out my two ounce Smilin' Bill Bucktail with a red pork rind attached to 100 feet of SS wire and a 15 foot leader of 50 pound mono. The rhythmic snapping of the jig began to warm my chilled torso when on the second pass a solid strike spun me sternward. The first bass of that day was a handsome 10 pound specimen, appreciated for its beauty and strength and equally prized for the three bucks it would bring at market. It was far from a hot bite, but the fishing was steady for about an hour or more before the sun finally creased through the curtain of sea smoke stacked up along the eastern horizon. As if on cue the restrained sunlight lifted squadrons of sea gulls off their damp roosts on East Island and directed them due east toward what appeared to be bird action along the breaking horizon. I'm usually reluctant to leave a steady bite for a gamble, yet on that day I took it. Halfway to the diving birds I spotted a few fish breaking dead ahead causing me to veer so as not to run over and spook them.

My second spinning rod was loaded with a surface popper but I didn't want to wrestle with treble hooks so I snapped on a Kastmaster with a single hook bucktail and let it fly. What followed was the best casting action I'd ever experienced up to that time. Stripers from eight to 12 pounds were slashing pods of baitfish and gorging to the point that they were puking up bait all over my cockpit. On the breath of that slight NE wind I drifted with that school for almost two miles catching stripers for just under two hours until the fish sounded. I never thought I would ever celebrate the desertion of fish until that moment of absolute exhaustion. There were over 25 bass piled up on the deck but because of my greed and wanton blood lust I lost as many if not more than I landed. The Kastmaster accounted for more than half of the linesiders and would have kept on catching if not for the dental apparatus of a passing yellow eye. Both spinners were bereft of leaders and lures, so with four live eels still contentedly sluggish in cracked ice I motored over to Warren's Point to make a few drifts. Sakonnet Harbormaster Jimmy Blades had been out tending lobster gear when those fish first showed and came over to socialize when the blitz was over. There was a cracked Atom plug tethered to the eye ring on his rod with an old Mitchell reel attached with black electrical tape. Although he was busy hauling gear, every time a school of bass came within range he let fly, but it appears they were not interested in

34

poppers. He had one 10 pound fish atop his motor box and reported he had lost a few more due to dull hooks.

I offered him one of my eels along with a 9/0 Eagle Claw snelled to a length of 50-pound mono which he graciously accepted. I picked up two larger bass in the 15 to 18-pound class on the remaining eels until the blues cut me off and I headed for the harbor. As I backed into my slip, Elsie Johnson who ran the Cove Market came over and told me that Jimmy had caught a 41-pound striper on an eel and sold her the fish which she was presently steaking for preferred customers. There was no resentment on my part because that hard working waterman deserved every break he caught. One of the greybeards from the Wilcox Fish Trap company walked over to view my catch and identified the baitfish as "Hardtails" a colloquial name for that form of sardine. I decided to sell my catch in New Bedford rather than Drapes in Fall River where word of that haul would cause the barstool anglers to vacate their seats and give chase. It was a bit of an inconvenience but well worth the trouble. I had almost eight straight days of lock and load fishing before that last best fall run I have ever participated in came to its abrupt conclusion. Even then it took three icy mornings of fishing in a frigid ocean devoid of life before I finally admitted it was over. After that there were some good years and some off years but fall fishing has always been as much about violent weather as numbers of fish moving through. Taking an honest look back I could have made much more money working, rather than fishing, but I am eternally grateful I didn't have the good sense to make that decision at the time.

WE CAN'T KEEP CATCHING IF WE DON'T RELEASE A FEW JUMBOS THAT GO ON TO SPAWN AND REPOPULATE THIS IMPORTANT SPECIES.

LEGENDS IN THEIR OWN MINDS

EGOS ON THE LOOSE

There's one in just about every tackle shop on the east coast and Bucko Brothers was no exception. Regular patrons will immediately recognize the overzealous advocate who pounces on you as soon as you walk in the door. The current overbearing occupant of Buckos at that time was a resident of a well-to-do suburb who we later learned had been booted out of upscale Thompson's Sporting Goods before taking up residence in the mill city bait shop. I had a few brushes (confrontations) with him causing him to ignore me whenever I walked in the shop. We were of different attitudes. He was in search of celebrity while attempting to fabricate a reputation as a fishing mentor while I was seeking anonymity and keeping a low profile. We were into incredible fishing in a very private location and I was looking out my rear view mirror to insure that our secret spot remained just that. During one of our altercations Stanley told the wannabe that if he spent as much time fishing as I did, rather than hanging around the shop trying to dispense unwanted advice, he just might learn something about catching stripers. That was an affront that would have sent most reasonable men packing but he brushed it off and continued to hold court eager for a novice to walk in the door so he could launch into his tutorial and gain their undying admiration for setting them on the right path.

During the years I observed him it was like a re-run of an old B-movie. Despite the numerous rebuffs to his overtures he doggedly continued his assaults on patrons. Stanley called him a deaf fanatic and Joe concurred with that designation and when the Bucko Brothers agreed on a label you could take it to the bank. The man might have been helpful to someone looking for guidance but his high handed method didn't sit well with most hopeful anglers. This was back in the days of the R.J. Schaeffer Saltwater Fishing Contest, a tourney that included eight states and several thousand fishermen all hunting for stripers and bluefish and competing for award pins, trophies and badges. One of the prized and most common awards was an oblong red enamel pin that was awarded to competing members who scored 100 or more points by catching striped bass over 15-pounds which was the minimum size for stripers. Back then if a member caught seven stripers of 15-pounds or four bass of 25-pounds they qualified for that pin. With so many competitors scoring well over a hundred points the Schaeffer directors raised the next plateau to 250-points and designated the aforementioned pin with a gold star to signify those anglers who attained that rank. It was a regular occurrence to meet numerous anglers with the plain awards pins and the few who proudly wore the pins with the gold star. The contest also awarded large gold plated merit badges as well as 50 and 60-pound pins for anglers who scored stripers in those respective weight classes.

Most of the award pins were worn on the front of fishing caps to identify contest participants and their rank. The wannabe high liner who hung his hat at Bucko's wore a long billed sword fisherman cap with the basic 100-point pin proudly displayed on the face of that hat. The pin was so shiny that it appeared he never wore his hat anywhere near saltwater or he polished it every night so he could display his Red Badge of achievement. At that time I possessed a modest collection of award pins but after witnessing my partner Russ losing his prized sword fisherman cap festooned with numerous 50-pounder and merit pins to Davy Jones locker I stripped my hat down to a single 250 point pin in order to minimize any impending losses. One late summer afternoon I was heading off to fish Newport with my buddy Joe who insisted on paying for the bait so I parked across the street from Buckos while he went in. As soon as he walked in the open door I watched the fanatic engage him. Much to the chagrin of the proprietors their uninvited guest's tactic was to ask the customer what they were fishing for then launch into a tutorial on what to buy and how to use it. At first Joe, who had never seen this guy before was amused but when the chap continued to flaunt his pin along with dispensing erroneous advice my fishing partner excused himself and walked back out to the car to retrieve his own hat. Joe had what he called a ceremonial cap that he wore to club meetings and events where we represented the Linesiders Bass Club of Fall River at sportsman's and trade shows. That cap was decorated with four 50-pounder pins and the super sixty pounder pin for the gigantic striper he'd caught fishing on my boat the previous season. He put on his shirt with the badges and awards from numerous fishing tourneys and headed back into the shop.

Joe Bucko said the Barrington braggart saw my friend coming and headed for the rest room but Stanley blocked the swinging gate leaving the man trapped as my pal descended upon him. I was tempted to leave the car and join in the exorcism but I grudgingly kept to my seat while Joe had the pretender for lunch. I can't tell you exactly what transpired but according to Stanley and Joe the braggart got his comeuppance in spades and that during the tirade his eyes were fixated on Joes highly decorated hat. We laughed all the way on the drive to Ruggles Avenue that night and according to Stan and Joe they didn't see their unwelcome tutor, who had been an almost daily visitor, again for weeks. The vast majority of fishermen I know and have met are competitive and often times very secretive individuals with a large segment that relish displaying their accomplishments. That is why every successful tournament promoter is aware of the importance of the contest specific T-shirts and patches that are favored by the competitive anglers. At every show and seminar the pins, patches and shirts tell a story of the anglers past, present and accomplishments to date. I have a section of my closet full of what professional anglers began to refer to as HERO attire. My hats and clothing have been supplied by sponsors to wear while working their subsidized events such as the fishing weekends at the Bass Pro Shops and Cabela's store promotions. The more understated shirts, caps and jackets are fine for fishing and casual dress while the practical clothing provided by the Fisherman and On The Water magazines are comfortable all season items I wear frequently much to my bride's chagrin.

I can recall a time when I would have given almost anything to own a hat or jacket encumbered with award pins and patches yet shortly after I achieved that goal I began to hear the words of my father whispered in my ear. "Son, when you become successful you won't have to tell or show people, others will do that for you." I have never forgotten that advice. When I think back to the early days of purchasing tackle on the cuff at Bucko's it brings back memories of a much simpler times. If I had hooks, bait, two bucks in my pocket and a full tank of gas in the Chevy wagon I was walking in tall cotton. Looking back on a much simpler time I realize just how much I miss those Sunday dinners around my mother's oval kitchen table where she served baked chicken with red roasted potatoes and a huge coil of chouricio in spicy burgundy gravy. FDR would have been proud of her kitchen. Today most of my plaques and trophies have been donated to the Boy Scouts or private trophy rooms and the pins, with the exception of a collection for my grandson, have been traded or sold to collectors. That was the epicenter of a bygone era during a period when the men and woman of the greatest generation lived, worked and raised their families. Tackle shop proprietor Stanley Bucko passed on at the age of 92 but he lives forever in the fond memories of thousands of fishermen who visited him at the bait shop on Second Street. His kid brother Joe still works in the tackle business every day at Bucko's Parts and Tackle, his son Mike's business on Stafford Road. Joe turned 90 a few years ago and has a much better memory and repertoire of jokes than I could ever hope for. I recently found an old New Bedford sword fisherman's cap in the basement with a tarnished 50-pounder pin stuck over the bill. I just might polish it up and take up residence at Buckos and see what kind of excitement and reactions that might bring.

THE AWARDS PINS FROM THE R.J. SCHAEFFER FISHING CONTEST WERE A MEANS OF IDENTIFYING A NOVICE FROM A SUCCESSFUL FISHERMAN. RUSS MALONE, PAUL CAPONE AND RONNIE SOARES WERE THE AUTHORS DECKMATES ON THE LONG TRIPS TO CUTTYHUNK. MANY OF THESE HERO HATS FLEW OUT OF THE COCKPIT AND WERE CLAIMED BY DAVEY JONES LOCKER.

COMPEITION OVER THE DECADES

THE GLORY DAYS OF STRIPER FISHING

The 1950's are famous for Rock-N-Roll, pegged pants, suede shoes and DA's but I'm certain historians left out one of the most important developments of that decade. The 50's were the era of the re-birth of the Striped Bass clubs that took up where the West Island, Cuttyhunk and Pasque Bass Clubs left off in the late 1800's. One of the major differences in these organizations was the fact that the former clubs were founded by wealthy sportsman at a time when bass stocks were declining. The contemporary clubs were primarily blue-collar organizations founded during an era, which will forever be cherished as the halcyon years of striped bass fishing. The Linesiders Bass Club of Fall River was founded in 1955 and competed in the famous R.J. Schaeffer Salt Water Fishing Contest. I became a member of that organization in 1958 as an ambitious kid who took over the duties of Fishing Committee Chairman and eventually the presidency until the membership matured and moved on to other pursuits when the club was eventually disbanded in the 1980's. That is just one of the reasons why sportsman's organizations need an infusion of women and children to become successful and enduring. We were a small but extremely talented collection of bass fisherman and almost every spring without fail took advantage of the fantastic live herring fishing in our inland rivers and bays.

This early run of large bass usually catapulted us into the early lead of the famous R.J. Schaeffer Salt-Water Fishing Contest, which at that time consisted of over 300 clubs from nine coastal states. As FCC Chairman I was always the first to view the monthly newsletter and standings in the contest and during the spring the Linesiders were always in the top 10 overall and one of the top three clubs in Massachusetts. Our leads were usually short-lived, lasting until the July tabulations when the Mass Striped Bass Association usually took over first place and held onto that favored position until the end of the year. The Massachusetts Striped Bass Association was founded in 1950 and I looked upon that organization with a grudging admiration yet the response from our membership when I revealed the contest standings at our monthly meetings was always who the hell are those MSBA guys? At that time the Linesiders had a membership of between 85 to 90 men and only a handful of women and of that number only 35 to 40 were active fishermen who registered stripers over the 15-pound minimum and contributed to the club's point total. The question of just who MSBA members were, was answered in the first person a few years later on a crisp October night at Cuttyhunk.

I had just tied up to the guide's dock after three hours of fantastic fishing under the shadow of Southwest bluff. We had the good sense never to publicly display our fish because showing up a Cuttyhunker who was making a living catching bass for clients with artificials lures was a difficult task. Despite my best efforts to conceal our catch the heavy canvas tarp would only stretch so far and several large tails protruded from under the cover. Although it was 3.00 AM you would never know it with the activity as the charter boats were coming in from fishing a tide while others headed out to fish the next. At that time two men stepped off one of the boats then walked over to us and struck up a conversation. The taller of the two was wearing a MSBA patch on his jacket (the first I'd ever seen) and asked how many fish we had so I told him it was just a very slow night without any embellishments or specifics. He smiled knowingly and said they were fishing with Captain Frank Sabatowski and were trolling nearby and in the moonlight they observed us hauling fish over the gunwale. Just then the impressive figure of Captain Sabby arrived and posed the same question. When I responded in kind he smiled and said he appreciated the fact that we didn't flaunt our catches and that was the reason he never chased me off the dock. Complying with his request we pulled the canvas off a catch of 15 bass, two of which broke the magical 50-pound barrier.

Sabby had informed his clients that he believed we were fishing live eels in the stones where the fish were holding tight at a time when the bass would not move out of the boulders to chase the huge plugs they were towing on heavy wire line. The MSBA member asked where he could buy some live eels and Sabby informed him they were very scarce and difficult to come by at that time of year. I'd been earning subsistence money for years potting my own eels and came to the island with an ample supply. Despite the fact that my competitive juices were intense and always flowing I learned that by assisting others I was sometimes helped in kind. If someone was experiencing a cold spell or a run of bad luck a suggestion, tip or perhaps the loan of a lure to help them out always provided a great deal of satisfaction. My philosophy was and still is that no one was ever going to catch my fish. I sold 10 eels for 30 cents each (a nickel more than I charged my fellow club members) to my new friends from Mass Bass and met them on the Dry Pigs the following morning as I headed back to Sakonnet. The angler with the MSBA patch lifted a hefty 50 inch fish that I estimated to be in the 55-pound range smiled and thanked me for my kindness. I wished him well, tipped my hat and pointed my bow in the direction of the mainland.

Mass Bass finished in first place in the state that year with the Linesiders a close second. I never did meet those fishermen again but over the years it was my good fortune to develop lasting friendships with many members of Mass Striped Bass when I spoke at their banquets and presented seminars at their meetings and shows. Since that time there is not a season that goes by that I do not meet with numerous people who fished the Schaeffer contest and we have enjoyed enduring friendship and great discussions. I still have a few of the awards, memorabilia and badges from what I consider the halcyon days of striper fishing and competition. In 2006 On The Water Magazine launched the Striper Cup which the recreational fishing community received with overwhelming enthusiasm. In that inaugural year we formed a team of ten men which I named the Linesiders Bass and Brew; a moniker which I derived from my old Linesiders club. Our modest roster of less than 10 men combined for a season where seven members were able to contribute to the point total that incredibly put us at the top of the heap on the very last day of the contest. There have been numerous changes and some fine tuning since that first year but our accomplishment demonstrates that dedicated and determined striped bass fishermen, no matter how many members they might have, are provided the opportunity to compete and benefit from the rivalry that a fishing contest promotes. There were seasons when I fished in as many as nine different competitions and found that the competitive edge made me a better fisherman. I'm somewhat uncomfortable using the term "fishing harder' because to outsiders that might convey that fishing is work rather than enjoyment; fishermen know what that term means. I have established that in circumstances such as my encounter with the Mass Bass members at Cuttyhunk decades ago we can compete and remain on friendly and in many cases on cooperative terms. Most fishermen I know benefit from the healthy competition a contest provides so get out there fish sensibly, keep safe and enjoy the fishing season.

THIS IS A COLLECTION OF SOME OF THE AUTHORS AWARD PINS AND BADGES FROM THE HEYDAY OF THE R.J. SCHAEFFER FISHING CONTEST. THE MERIT BADGES AND THE 50 POUNDER PINS WERE THE MOST PRIZED. AT THE TIME THEY ISSUED A SUPER SIXTY POUND PATCH RATHER THAN A 60 POUND PIN.

FIRST KEEPERS

WHERE WHEN AND HOW

When the hand gripping your reel seat is too cramped from the cold to lift up and wipe the icicle from your nose that implies it might be a bit early to be out prospecting for stripers. Every spring for as long as I can remember the aforementioned conditions cause me to make the same promise which I consistently break every year. As I've admitted in the past, long before we have any right to expect a fresh run fish to be in residence the urge to wade the frigid waters of our rivers and bays overcomes years of personal experience and an historical abundance of common sense. Casting lures along the edge of the bogs and the stems of emerging eelgrass of backwater herring runs, tidal rivers and salt creeks is much more about speculation and compulsion than catching fish. Stripers are not the property of Connecticut, Rhode Island, Massachusetts or New Hampshire they are migrants, the gypsies of our waterways. These fish travel from the warm brackish waters of the south to the icy cold rivers of Maine providing gratification and food along their way. These beautiful seven striped fish visit with us just long enough to entangle us in their web. They are like the wild girl (or boy) you met during your summer vacation. After an all too brief fling they break your heart by leaving as they begin their return migration to entertain, feed and capture the hearts of thousands of anglers who await them on their westward journey.

I fell in love with stripers the day I saw old man Tito haul one up out of the water onto the granite shoulders that supported the old Brightman Street Bridge. It was silver, striped and gleamed iridescent in the early morning sun but the glimpse was brief as the old man slipped it into the wet burlap sack that held his white perch and tautog. In those days you always kept at least a rock toss away from those old curmudgeons who didn't want anything to do with inquisitive kids. Smitten by the sight of that bass gave me the courage to call out and ask what kind of fish he'd just caught. His response was "it's a choggie (cunner) now get the hell out of here." I thought that if he could catch one of those handsome fish on a green crab my chances of duplicating his success with a large seaworm should be at least as good. From that day on I was fascinated by the linesider and 50 years later this species still causes me to behave in a manner that responsible individuals fail to understand. As cold as it was that evening I knew that when the tide changed any bass holding in a downstream slough would begin to move uptide to the herring run under these low light conditions. Rubbing my hands and stamping my feet to promote circulation I knew that somewhere close to the tackle shop the kibitzers were holding court in one of the neighborhood taverns or pizza parlors. They were sipping pictures of beer and supping on warm food while I was attempting to keep my bodily fluids from freezing.

These lads knew that a few other guys and I were fishing and as soon as they got word that we hit a fish or two they would join the fray. Not this year. My tolerance for the cold finally overcame my desire and I headed home for the comfort of the rocking chair in front of the woodstove. There is never any shortage of calls at my home particularly during fishing season and that night was no exception. I perused the list discounted the non-fishermen and discussed strategy with other working anglers. No one had scored yet but it would only be a matter of time. A few days later on the evening of April 19th, 2002, to be exact, Joy Nelson and Mike Kanilias joined me to welcome a substantial school of three to five pound stripers on the Coles River. The very first place fresh run schoolies usually show is the Connecticut River and the West Wall at Point Judith, but a former editor who chides me about my aversion to crowds knows that between the lobster pots and the flying plugs and jigs that is one place I avoid. I'd rather catch one fish alone or with a good companion than a dozen in a crowd. This discussion is about keepers but you won't usually find them until the schoolies lead the way as the larger fish work their way into shallow waters by honing in on the scent of herring in their brackish water runs. Two of the most productive locations for early schoolies (that is mid to late April) in my haunts are the Coles River Bridge at Route 103 and the Lees River which was quite a bit warmer due to the thermal discharge of the Brayton Point Power plant which was another hot spring location. The backwaters of the Kikimuit River up along the holes and the bogs next to the Route 103 dam in Warren is another early season location worth a few casts at the top of the flood tide.

If I had to select just one place within the scope of my entire angling range to catch the very first legitimate keeper of the year I'd have to choose the Warren River in the East Bay of Rhode Island. Year after year this area produces not only the first of the legal fish but also some bass of very respectable proportions. Contrary to popular yet misleading intelligence during the peak of spring herring runs the big fish are not found along cold and barren ocean ledges and reefs but way up in estuaries that many anglers would never think of as foraging locations for trophies. I do not presume to suggest you cannot catch a heavyweight along a beach or rocky ocean shoreline because that is the route they travel along the coast before turning into our rivers and bays to feed on the herring and later on the menhaden that usually follow. I'll conclude by saying you won't find me or any of my colleagues sitting by a sand spike along the ocean on a May or early June night. We will be up in the rivers and shallow bays fishing holes where bass to 44-pounds were waiting in ambush last year for the herring to drop back on the falling tides and that is why the convergence of an area like the Warren and Barrington Rivers is so productive. So much so that fishermen anchoring up or tying off on moorings live line herring block the channel and access to the slips and gas docks casting dirty looks at anyone who respectfully idles by trying to make their way upriver. In earlier years we've trolled up bass in the 30-pound class at this location which is known as Tyler Point and anyone who has travelled the bike path (that spans the two bridges) from late April to mid June has seen bass in the 20-pound class lying on the cement deck, the casualties of a live or chunked herring. If you direct your efforts in the rivers that support herring runs you might find keeper bass, particularly if you offer them a live or fresh chunk of herring, menhaden or mackerel. It would be impossible to list all the places we have taken our first early season legal stripers but the key is the aforementioned rivers.

Despite our predictions, past history, expectations or the forecasts of the most knowledgeable meteorologists, Mother Nature has her own timetable and a way of humbling even the most scientific theories. After years of chasing stripers in my own backyard I'm acutely aware that I've never caught a legal sized bass in this skinny water before May 7th although I've lost a few that straightened hooks designed to hold schoolies. The water is beginning to come to life with grass shrimp scurrying underfoot and chubs exploding out from their cover in the stubby eelgrass where casting for bass should never have been a perfunctory exercise. Watching workmen performing repetitive tasks causes me to think of anglers dragging a popping plug across the surface with the same speed and rhythm and no sense as to what it is they are trying to imitate. The lure should mimic a wounded baitfish, struggling on the surface presenting a tempting target for hungry stripers arriving after long migrations. Although you can't beat a live or fresh chunk of herring early in the season when the water is cold light plastic swim baits worked slowly along the bottom will produce fish of all sizes. Save the topwater lures for those unseasonably warm days when bass are more likely to come to the surface to catch a meal. While I wouldn't categorize casting for bass as work, I know you can't catch fish unless your line is in the water. From the period of early May right through the end of June some of the largest bass of the season will be feeding in skinny water close to the mouths of herring runs and tidal rivers. Fishing these areas under low light conditions should continue to result in consistent catches of larger stripers.

AN EARLY SPRING JUMBO CAUGHT UP IN THE SHALLOWS AT THE MOUTH OF THE POND BRIDGE ROAD HERRING RUN IN THE LOWER SAKONNET RIVER.

HIDING IN PLAIN SIGHT

THE REWARDS OF A CONSCIENTIOUS FISHERMAN

Looking up I saw the distinctive bow wake of a boat bearing down on me which was adequate notice to call for the anchor to be hauled before I moved off the spike we were fishing. Andy wasn't thrilled with the prospect of hauling back 120 feet of anchor line but he was accustomed to the drill so he heaved and hauled while grumbling about poachers and claim jumpers as I released a sub-legal tog and started the engine. By the time the boat was upon us we were about a hundred yards off the spike with our bare hooks 15 feet off the bottom to insure that even a suicidal sea bass wouldn't attack our rigs. The men in the other boat acted as though we weren't even there. One of them told their skipper he was certain that we had been closer to the green and white lobster pot while another passenger suggested we were out quite a bit further. They ran a few circles around us with their eyes glued to their chart recorder looking for the pile of fish they were certain was nearby. They were close, but close only counts in horseshoes and hand grenades and we were amazed that they didn't even drop lines over the side to test the waters. After a few turns and more grumbling they blew a hole in the water and headed off to bother some other unsuspecting fisherman that had taken the time to scout out a location rather than jump into a site that was already occupied.

Before you indict me for claiming ownership to public waters I would remind you that there is such a thing as angling etiquette, something I learned while I was rowing water logged skiffs and long before I ever took the tiller of an outboard motor. We gave everyone a wide berth unless we were invited and I recall plenty of invitations extended by other fishermen who were returning a favor. Back in those days we fished more for food than we did for sport yet we shared our good fortune with those who were seldom reluctant to return the favor. Today, with few exceptions, there seems to be a me first attitude which usually wears pretty thin with those of us who invest the time, effort and fuel to locate fish and search for other areas that might produce. It wouldn't be so objectionable if the offenders actually tried to locate fish holding structure on their own but that would take effort that many claim jumpers might consider work, something we refer to as paying our dues. This discussion was prompted by a conversation at the Westport, MA boat ramp some time ago. We had been out fishing one full hour before the late 6:30 AM sunrise and only had one 17-pound striper in the cooler. There were plenty of bass on the rockpiles with the best casting located around the white water breaking over the boulders however most of those fish were in the 6 to 10-pound class with a few bluefish in the mix. After sunrise we scouted a few deeper rockpiles until we found a few tautog holding on a spike in 35-feet of water. We were scratching a few leather lips with a ratio of one keeper for every eight sub-legal fish we caught when another boat approached.

We had just released two small fish as they came alongside and asked how we were doing. I replied that there were very few legal fish but that did not seem to deter them as they fumbled with their anchor and heaved it, rather than taking care to set it downwind of my boat. In less than a minute they were fending their boat away from my gunwale and all fishing ceased as we held them off while the man in the bow attempted to retrieve their anchor. In an inevitable episode of Murphy's Law their anchor fouled my anchor line which required me to haul my anchor and lose our secure bite over that prime location. Once we untangled the lines I headed out of the area while the other boat attempted to anchor over the location we had just vacated. Three hours later after hunting for fish over several more locations we returned to the harbor with the lone striper and two legal tautog. As luck would have it the boat that we tangled with pulled up to the dock right behind us. The boat owner asked how we fared and I told him we only managed one legal striper and two medium tautog but we looked around and found a few more holes that might be productive at some time in the future. The man (I'm reluctant to refer to him as a fisherman) told me he seldom burned precious fuel looking for places to fish because it was easier to look for other boats and fish close (hopefully not as close to others as he was to me) to them where he projected a reasonable expectation of success. That is just the attitude that turns fishermen away from attempting to help others who are only interested in short cuts.

While this conversation was taking place a Westport resident who I met on the river over a dozen years ago was about to launch his boat and came over to say hello and ask how we had done. Because he has always been courteous to everyone he meets on the water I waved him over to us one day when we were into a very productive bite of good sized tautog. Over the years he has reciprocated with information on his experiences and observations on the water and we are both more successful fishermen because of our alliance. Because of what appears to be the prevailing attitude it's become a literal pain in the neck but an absolute necessity for hard working fishermen to keep a 360-degree watch to prevent being ambushed. A few years ago I watched one group of anglers fishing what was once a very productive area for bass. They were catching fish when another boat came up to them and they continued fishing obviously thinking only of the moment. Later that season I met that man in the first group at the ramp and he complained that he was seldom able to fish that location because the second boat began heading out in the dark and anchoring up and chumming that location. Over a period of several weeks I passed that area and observed anywhere from two to five boats anchored up over what was once a very productive trolling location that had been lost for the season.

When you take into consideration that the ocean is so huge it seems incredible to me that most of the boats are usually concentrated in such a small area. In light of these situations I began leaving the harbor two hours before first light which some people might consider to a be a bit extreme to get a shot at that spot and cull a bass out of there which certainly beats fishing with the crowds. I will usually help someone who displays the initiative to help themselves and in turn might be able to bring something to the table. However, like the debt relief program that was being debated in congress I don't feel obligated to bail out people who abused their credit and are now hoping that we pay their bills. It's not a very complicated situation it's all about common sense and treating others as we would have others treat us. In the long run respecting another fisherman's space can pay big dividends in the future because good behavior seldom goes unrewarded.

THE AUTHOR'S SON CHARLIE WITH A 1975 HEAVYWEIGHT THAT WAS THE RESULT OF A MUTUAL COOPERATION PACT WITH HIS FRIEND FREDDY ST LOUIS.

PHILOSOPHICAL DIFFERENCES

A WELCOME CHANGE OF PACE

He claimed the smile on her face began to materialize after she sipped her second glass of wine but I knew better. It was the unexpected change of scenery, breaking away from what had become a stale routine although I'll admit the wine and fresh salt air didn't hurt a bit. Her normal Friday afternoon routine was to drive the children to her sister's house, wait for my friend to arrive home from work then head to the same restaurant before taking in a movie. There was nothing wrong with that except that it got stale after a while and neither of them thought the other was bored so they never complained or discussed their monotonous routine. Earlier in the summer the wife had asked and was granted a large favor. She asked me to hoodwink her husband into thinking we were going to join them for dinner so she could surprise him with a milestone birthday party. She and my wife collectively worked on the arrangements and he was so tired that evening that he really had no suspicions when I asked if he would mind if I stopped by a restaurant to pick up a gift certificate (which he incorrectly assumed was for him) then left him waiting in the car. By the time he finally decided to come looking for me he walked into what he still refers to as one of the best nights of his life.

It was a great party and his wife agreed that she owed me "big time" for helping her pull it off. His bride was a city girl from a well-to-do family who had never discouraged nor encouraged his penchant for fishing, however, she didn't care for the way his clothes looked and smelled when he came home from a trip and she wasn't bashful about expressing her displeasure. Over the years my friend fished less and less primarily due to the long hours required to run his business and the precious little time he dedicated to his two children. He was good company and it was depressing to see him so tired and although he attempted to disguise it, so dissatisfied. During that particular season he had not embarked on a single fishing trip and I did my best to tone down the rhetoric whenever he called to ask how the fishing was. He was at a point in his life and marriage where he was living vicariously through me. It was late September when I suffered through a week of squalls and ugly weather before I relented and took a client surf fishing at South Shore in Little Compton rather than have him return home to the dusty Midwestern plains fishless after three cancellations and rescheduling. We hit the beach that night with a stiff southwester in our faces arriving early to cast artificials before we fished cut bait on the bottom while tossing surface swimmers into the breakers.

The fish gods smiled on us that night particularly for my client who had never caught a fish from anything but a boat and he experienced the joys of surf fishing for the first time. He hooked a fish, a good bass on his third cast and the surface action lasted from an hour before sunset right up to the low slack water when tired and aching we walked back to the truck and headed out to locate a diner serving coffee and pie. I was bone tired but content with the fact that the man went home happy with a bag of fillets so I planned to take the following night off. During the day I thought about my friend who had not so much as wet a line that season and decided to call him to share in my good fortune. It was Friday, his date night, so I called his wife and discussed my plan with her. She was reluctant at first but she knew how hard he'd been working lately and more importantly how much he'd enjoy a night of fishing even if he didn't catch a fish. She agreed before I told her we were double dating that night and when she tried to beg off I called in my marker so she agreed to suffer through what she envisioned as a cold damp night huddled up in the Jeep waiting for her penance to be over. According to the rules of nature (including Murphy's Law) the 21 fish we'd caught the night before during a late summer blitz had moved on to another spot and although we managed to catch a few schoolies, one keeper and three bluefish my objective was not about catching fish but giving my disheartened friend a much needed change of pace He was willing but reluctant to break what he referred to as their normal routine but when I informed him I'd obtained clearance from his wife he began to sound upbeat although he threatened me with bodily harm if she had a miserable time and took it out on him.

That night she caught her very first schoolie she stepped into the water with her new jogging shoes never complaining a bit. It wasn't the rare steaks and delicious chops, the inexpensive red wine or the cheese and crackers that lifted her spirits it was the brilliant sunset which she seldom had time to appreciate, the calming sound of the pounding surf and the warmth from the charcoal fire she huddled around while interrogating my bride as to whether she really enjoyed this type of a night out or came along just to please me. My sympathetic wife told her that at first she went fishing out of a sense of duty to keep me company and in compensation for the many chick flicks, family outings and social gatherings I suffered through to make her happy. Originally it began as a case of philosophical differences until she began to enjoy the solitude of fishing on the beach rather than waiting in line 45 minutes for a table at a busy restaurant on a Friday night. For a change I did the rough cooking while she read or if it was a comfortable night she'd take up station alongside me and we'd enjoy a conversation while the surf licked at our feet. It was by no means a regular practice but she began to enjoy it and started to prepare side dishes to compliment my inept grilling as well as occasionally inviting another couple along. My friend's wife actually had a good time that evening so much so that she called her sister and asked if the children could sleep over so we could extend our stay at the ocean. My long-suffering friend was ecstatic. While I was cleaning the bass and blues his enthusiastic wife pitched in with the chore, helping me bag fish and even requesting a few fillets to share with her sister. For the first time in the past few years we saw the spark in her eyes and the warm smile that was her trademark as she turned to shoot us a wink. I'd like to tell you my friend bought a boat or that he and his wife became surf-fishing regulars but that was not the case. Twice more before the end of the season they joined us and we had a great time despite not catching a single fish other than a sand shark on one occasion. Fishing is a sport that is responsible for more hard feeling, separations and divorces than football, golf, baseball and basketball because it's not something you can enjoy from your living room sofa. Our friends still go out on Friday nights but they switch restaurants visit the beach with the kids and are much more considerate of each other's needs than they were when they were stuck in their predictable rut. You might not be able to talk your wife into a surf fishing trip, particularly in the spring or fall when it's downright chilly once the sun sets but a change of pace is beneficial for any relationship. My friend continues to work hard, spends quality time with the wife and kids but they also sneak off to South Shore Beach and Gooseberry Island on occasion to watch the sun set, barbecue and catch up on what's really important in their lives in a very relaxed and enjoyable atmosphere. Several months later my friend confided that prior to our initial trip his wife had suggested they see a marriage councilor to attempt to rekindle the flame they experienced throughout the early part of their marriage. Although I haven't any experience in marriage therapy I do know couples who've tried everything to save a failing relationship, bared their souls and suffered in the process by spawning a more divisive relationship. The couple we were certain was headed for trouble or a break-up is now closer than ever and I like to think that fishing trip played a small role in the transformation that helped to save their relationship. Perhaps it's time for you to take your wife, girlfriend or significant other fishing- just don't forget a comfortable chair, the wine and a warn blanket. Catching a fish won't hurt a bit.

ONLY THE LUCKY

TAKE ALL THE LUCK YOU CAN GET BUT NOTHING BEATS EXPERIENCE

The last thing I expected was for Artie to open the cover of the fish box. Prior to entering the harbor he was reminded to keep the lid on our catch so as not to gather any unwanted attention and he nodded in affirmation. Not twenty minutes later the cover was off and my friend was basking in the glory of an audience admiring our box full of stripers. This was not just any day it was a Sakonnet Sunday when every working class stiff from Fall River to New Bedford with a few bucks to spare packed the kids in the car and headed up the narrow two lane to the end of the road where the scent of saltwater and cool ocean breeze escaped to restore their sense of liberty. If the pilgrims were particularly affluent they might add an order of French fries and a thirty five cent tall Narragansett to their order of clam cakes and chowder. It was always crowded at the Point on weekends but it was not the tourists I was worried about. The incident that prompted Artie to open the cooler was initiated by three youthful anglers who had just returned from the scale house at the Wilcox Fish trap company where a man fishing the breakwater caught and weighed an eight pound striper. Not to be outdone my friend responded by opening what turned out to be Pandora's Box by displaying our catch to the masses.

Unbeknown to Artie the boat that followed us out of the harbor and began trolling outside the first traps had just returned and their crew was among the spectators. They had been trolling the gravel bottom from the breakwater over to Newport and back again presenting their lures over barren water. Their five hour effort did not produce a single bite so when the skipper looked down into my fish box and ogled our catch his first words were "boy, your guys are really lucky." Now you can call me Charley or even late for dinner but please don't call me lucky. The lucky tag might not offend some folks and might even seem like a compliment to some but not to me. If you invested as much time and capital in fishing as I have you might even take that as an affront. Don't get me wrong; I'll take all the luck I can get and as often as it breaks my way, but the man who called me lucky had about as much chance of catching stripers as the waitress from the Fo'cs'le that sat on the back porch overlooking the water shucking the quahogs

58

for the clam chowder. If I and most other fisherman set with only luck on their side our chances of success are negligible and that trip would almost certainly result in a long boring boat ride. I would be happy to spend the remainder of my fishing career without being referred to as lucky but I'm well aware that is not going to happen. Quite some time ago I hung up my rods on Halloween eve after catching nothing larger than schoolie sized stripers during the previous week. Four days later I called home from a Maine deer camp at which time my bride informed me that a reader had called to report that he had landed a 54-pound striper on an eel fishing in our mutual waters. Was that fisherman lucky? The only chance of luck in play was the size of the fish.

A few years ago I drove to Westport Harbor to water test the new Carolina Striper skiff from Eagle Marine that Lee Woltman took delivery of over that past week. Conditions were less than ideal with a snotty southwest wind colliding with a strong outgoing tide at the mouth of the river. That entrance can appear daunting and that day was no exception. We guided the boat up and over the turbulence and out past Halfmile Rock where the seas subsided somewhat but not quite enough for the trip to the ledges north of Cuttyhunk. We fished the area out to Quicksand Point where the alligator blues jumped all over our tubes and chomped on our live eels until we discontinued feeding the precious sea worms to those alligators. In the meantime the winds increased leaving the surface a turmoil of white water and windswept waves. Lee was more than happy with the way his new boat handled the seas and was ready to call it a day until I made a suggestion. There was one place I knew of, a location that usually produced under these conditions when strong winds and a falling tide created the rips where stripers reigned supreme. It was a gamble he was willing to take so I pointed the bow towards our destination into a vortex of wind and waves and with a sea breaking off our starboard beam. There was not a drop of bluefish blood left on the decks when we arrived and began our first drift. The boat was equipped with the necessary Coast Guard equipment and safety gear but we were without a sea anchor which forced us to power drift by using the engine to slow what was a very fast drift. On the very first pass I hooked up with a 33-pound striper that was reluctant to give up the bottom and shortly thereafter my deckmate caught a fish in the 20-pound class. The next two drifts I hooked and lost two very good fish but on the third Lee set the hook on a huge heavyweight that proceeded to tear line from the spool of his new reel.

That massive striper took him into the rocks where I gave chase. Anyone who has ever navigated the Gooseberry slot and the rips around Hens and Chickens is well aware of just how intimidating that stretch of water can be and it was not any different on that afternoon. We shipped water over the stern and when I got stuck between waves we took a few buckets of green water over the bow. That was when those watertight decks and scuppers along with a reliable bilge pump come in handy, not to mention the positive foam floatation and non sinking hull. After we loaded that bass into the cooler we made two more drifts but it was evident that whatever fish that had been feeding in that hole dispersed after the excitement or were recovering from a toothache. There are numerous observations about the role of luck in fishing but I have my own theory. You will never catch a 50 if you are fishing over 20's and that is where the luck or the law of averages comes in. On that bumpy afternoon there were only a certain number of stripers feeding in that hole and they ranged in size from about 20 to 40 pounds. Did that 47 give chase to my bait and did the 33 beat her to it? That we will never know but I hold fast to the theory that the only luck involved was in the size of the fish. The successful equation for that day was a seaworthy boat, experienced anglers who knew what to use, where to use it and possessed the tackle that was up to the task at hand. So many fishermen believe that if they knew where to find bass they might be successful. Not so. You not only have to find them, you have to tempt or convince them, and then you have to beat them in a battle on their home turf, on their own terms. How much luck was involved in our Wednesday afternoon foray and was it luck that saved the day? I already know the answer but that is something for you to decide.

LEE WOLTMAN WITH THE 47 POUNDER HE CAUGHT WITH CHARLEY.

CHAPTER III

CONFLICTS

CONSISTENTLY SCORING STRIPERS IN THE TROPHY CLASS REQUIRES A COMMITMENT TO EMPLOYING THE VERY BEST IN TACKLE AND TACTICS.

CLAIM JUMPERS ON THE LOOSE

WE WERE ALWAYS LOOKING OVER OUR SHOULDERS

The circumstances seldom change; it just takes on a different manifestation. Back then they were playing the same old waiting game as they positioned their abundant backsides onto the bar stools each season on those chilly early spring evenings, quaffing their drafts and the occasional cheap whiskey boilermakers, smoking cigarettes, consuming suspect bar food and watching the only color TV in the entire neighborhood. Every so often one of those lazy fishermen would walk over to the window and glance toward the bait and tackle shop looking for any encouraging signs of activity. It was mid April and much too uncomfortable outdoors for men content with having someone else do their heavy lifting so they sat and waited for news of the arrival of the first bright run schoolies. They knew the kids were out there somewhere, more than likely fishing up inside of the Kikimuit, probably having made the long slippery trek out to the bar to cast their homemade poppers or buck tailed Hopkins into the rip on the incoming tide.

One old timer recalled that it was on a similar cold drizzly evening last year when the duo returned after dark with a burlap sack full of fresh run schoolies ranging from three to five pounds that earned them the loot for first fish of the year pool. That long ago evening ended with no sign of the boys so one by one the loafers emptied their glasses and walked home to wait another day for news of the arrival of the seven striped fish. Little did they know that shortly after the lights went out in the bait shop the boys drove around the back of the building and entered through the rear door? The bait shop was the only place around with a walk in cooler they could store their bass in until they brought them to market before work the following morning. That chess game continued throughout the season and in fact in subsequent year's right up to the present day. There were few well kept secrets back then and considerably fewer today and rather than tavern hangers on it's the internet junkies that have taken over and every fisherman's move is tracked by thousands of eyes and millions of key strokes.

There will always be the optimistic pioneers who venture out in search of the unpredictable scouts that execute the miracle of migration while the claim jumpers are still reluctant to subject their person to the elements that have yet to escape the grip of a hard winter. No one with a whit of common sense would wade out into frigid water to cast a lure for a fish that might yet be hundreds of miles away, but then again, none of my acquaintance has ever suggested that fishermen were a sensible lot. Decades later everything remains pretty much the same except for the price of the libations and the dissemination of the intelligence gathering. Internet chat rooms have replaced the taverns and now these unknown heroes with untraceable names can brag about suspect and unproven past accomplishments or attempt to destroy the credibility or reputation of others without fear of retribution. There is something about talking to another fisherman face to face that requires a certain degree of honesty; however hiding behind a nickname- usually one that enhances their status-makes it easier to gossip and exaggerate. And so it is the optimistic anglers go forth in search of the first schoolies not for recognition or rewards but to experience the quiet times as they shed the cloak of winter before the beaches and jetties become crowded once they have completed their mission and the claim jumpers rush to take up positions beside them.

I bear no malice toward anyone who chooses to remain in the comfort of their home or a friendly watering hole because there have been so many raw spring nights when I questioned my sanity for wading in 40-degree waters shivering and wishing I were at home by the woodstove sipping a warm beverage. Yet the next night with the weather little if any better we find ourselves back out there searching and hoping for a sign. It could be animated baitfish or perhaps a bird hovering over structure; signs that provide a glimmer of hope that warm the body and comfort the soul. Every year, usually from mid to late April the first scouts arrive in the backwaters of the Coles River where the dark bottom, bright sun and the shallow water combine to increase the water temperature and attract fish into this bait rich area. Last year it was once again on the 19th a date which has proved to be dependable, when the first schoolies arrived to feast on the emerging grass shrimp and plump chubs that seek refuge in the undercut bogs and trenches of the waterway. That night I was alone and for good reason. For the past week I had aggravated the already distressed rotator cuff of my right shoulder to a point that if I turned my arm in bed I was aroused by a sharp pain.

The lady of the house suggested I give my shoulder a break and catch up on selecting the final photos for the current book I was working on. Less than a half hour into that exercise I walked to the kitchen window and noticed two egrets and our old friend Ichabod the blue heron working bait on the opposite shore. The persistent northwest wind had died so I headed to the basement where my boots and fishing gear had been discarded the night before, quickly dressing before descending the stairs to the beach. Before I negotiated the steep banking I surveyed the river and noticed activity along the edge of the rip forming over the boulders just west of our beach. A tepid sun was visible through a slit in the overcast as I fastened a six inch Hogy to the 20-pound leader material. Four fan casts loosened up my shoulder and produced nothing other than a painful reminder of why I had suspended my activities the night before. Just then a riffle at the boulder; not a break or a swirl but a minor disturbance caused me to turn and cast the light lure in that direction. No matter how many times I have engaged in this pursuit I never fail to become energized so that first sign of life caused me to retrieve much too fast and just as I lifted the lure from the water I caught the flash of a striper as it turned and bolted back to deeper water.

My first reaction was to cast back to that spot but I knew the fish did not have the time to reestablish its station so I walked 15 yards to the cove and made a few unproductive casts before quietly walking back and preparing what was to be the most important cast of that new season. A flip of the rod placed the tiny lure out in front of the striper's lie and my retrieve brought it around but within sight of the little striper laying in ambush. The last thing I wanted to do was to spook the fish by dropping the lure atop its immediate hide. The wriggling white Hogy did not make it past the rock before the bass smacked it in the head and felt the bite of the sharp hook. With very little water to negotiate in the little bass came to the surface, shook its head and dove for the faster water of the rip. The light rod bowed against the influence of the diminutive striper but after two short runs the fish came easily to hand. Over a lifetime of fishing I've been blessed with the gift of numerous stripers but every spring, the first bright run fish I liberate, ranks right up there with the trophies and tournament winners because that catch means I've survived another winter and hopefully been granted another season in the pursuit of our revered striped bass.

I didn't make another cast. Leaning back against the overturned skiff at the base of our stairs I looked out on what was one of the most perfect of early spring evenings. The Pine Point osprey cast a shadow on the river's sun streaked surface as it headed for its nest with a herring clutched in its talons. The fish Gods were smiling that evening and the pain in my shoulder was no longer a concern. If there is a reward for persistence it is sharing the fruits of my efforts with friends and readers who would do the same for me. That night with the exhilaration of a resurrected fisherman I spread the news. The bass are in!

HOW EARLY IS TOO EARLY? THE AUTHOR (RIGHT) AND HIS PAL JOE WERE OUT PROSPECTING FOR STRIPERS DURING A SPRING SNOWSTORM LONG BEFORE THE LOAFERS, WHO WAITED FOR SOMEONE ELSE TO DO THE PROSPECTING, GOT OFF THEIR LAZY BUTTS AND WET A LINE.

WHO LET THE DOGS OUT

BE CAREFUL WHAT YOU SAY AND HOW YOU ACT THE WATER

He obviously didn't see Dan's truck and boat parked in the lot behind the building but he definitely noticed that large presence of a man sitting at the bar with a few friends on that stormy Friday evening. Second only to family; fishing was everything to those men and after putting in 48 long hard hours during the week they looked forward to their Friday night fishing forays which usually lasted from sundown to sunrise. Many of the men fished the surf but Dan and a few others worked the inshore waters along the ocean between Newport and Westport Harbor in small outboard powered boats. Dan was one of the members of a local fishing club who owned an 18-foot center console that he trailered from Newport to the Cape Cod Canal where he launched at the Sandwich Marine Basin in the early spring and fall to catch the mackerel and pollock runs at either end of the season. He was a genial man not given to boasting or excessive drinking and the only time I ever heard him curse was when someone went out of their way to provoke him. The hound that walked in the door of the neighborhood tavern was also kept off the water by the foul weather and he was obviously there to order takeout from the highly regarded kitchen staff. I was facing Dan and didn't see the guy walk in the door but Dan slammed his draft down and came off his stool like he'd been electrocuted. I turned in time to see a pale faced individual standing in the tavern wearing an expression of terror on his face and appearing as though his feet were nailed to the floor.

"You son of a bitch; sooner or later I knew I was going to catch up with you. What do you have to say to me now?"Dan shot past me with a speed belying the size of the man and had the intruder by the lapels of his jacket before his stool stopped spinning. Two of his friends attempted to pull him away but he was totally unaware of their presence. "Go ahead and repeat what you said to me on the water." The man stammered and trembled, and despite my friendship with Dan, I almost felt sorry for the endangered man. Dan was shaking him and speaking in a low soft growl. "Your fast boat won't get you out of trouble today you cowardly dog." Jimmy knew Dan better than me and he stepped in and whispered something in Dan's ear. The big man smiled and released his grip as the perpetrator spun on his heels and was out the door in a flash. Dan let out a roar. "Do you think I scared the hell out of him?" Jim replied that he couldn't make an observation on that but either Dan spilled a drink on him or the man pissed his pants. The bartender was smiling from ear to ear and set up a round of drafts on the house. The gentle giant finally sat down and the story began to unfold. For the past two seasons Dan had been hounded by that interloper and his crew and it seemed that no matter where he was whenever he hooked up those snoops were not far behind. During their last encounter the interlopers climbed right up on his lines and one of Dan's crew lost it. After warning them to keep out of plugging range they swooped in with their much faster boat and in the crudest of terms they challenged his manhood. Neither Dan nor his deckmates ever mentioned this incident us so when we saw what transpired in the tavern we were surprised.

There may be shortcuts to elevating your rank in the angling world but hounding successful fishermen is not one of them. When I first began fishing on my own there were a few sharpies working the same area I was concentrating in and I can honestly admit there were times when I was so hungry and desperate I was tempted to shadow them to their honey holes but I didn't want to alienate those fellow fisherman I was sharing this habitat with. There is not a man alive (or dead) who can accuse me of ever jumping into their space; it's just not something I do. I bit my tongue and kept my distance until one day I was moving from Easton Point to Brenton Reef when I looked into a gnarly cove where I had managed to scratch a few decent fish on eels. The jet Black bass boat was in there again and I could see the two men aboard were fighting fish. That skipper was a high hook and although I had never made his acquaintance we had waved in passing and on a few nights when we were both working eels and casting plugs along Ocean Drive in Newport when he would blink his lights to signal he was in an area I was moving by. On this late fall afternoon he began waving and I thought he might have lost power or be in some kind of trouble so I moved in cautiously. "The first words he ever spoke to me were "tie on a big swimmer and lay one up close to the breakers." I was hesitant to get in that close to him but he kept on waving me over so I followed his suggestion and snapped on a big pearl Creek Chub swimmer. That plug hit the water and didn't move more than five feet before it was attacked by a 20-pound striper on steroids. As I was fighting the fish he lifted up a striper that had to be in the mid 50-pound class and gave me the thumbs up. We cautiously and quietly worked that shallow cove until the fish moved out and when he called me over I got to peek into his cockpit where at least 20 big bass from 20 to over 50-pounds were stacked up against the stern tiller station.

I ended up with five fish from 20 to 34-pounds; all on plugs, and thanked him for his kindness. I will never forget his response to my expression of gratitude. "Kid, I've been fishing this piece of water for 45 years and I've had just about every dog with a fishing rod hound me because they were too lazy to learn and find fish on their own. For the past two years I've watched you move along this stretch and never once bother me, even when it was obvious I was into fish so I thought it was time for me to say thank you." Wow, I could not believe my ears. No, we never became best friends but on at least two occasions I was able to return the favor. We were both market fishing at the time and one day I was into lock and load fishing trolling my tubes on Elbow Ledge when I spotted him up inside Satuest Cove. I was all alone and didn't have the benefit of a radio so I went in and hailed him. He followed me to the ledge where we both continued to catch fish; he began snapping wire line and Smilin' Bills while I continued with the tubes until the sun set. He came over to my boat and handed me a brand new six volt waterproof lantern of which he claimed to have two. It was a quantum leap from the rusting metal Ray-O-Vac flashlight I was using at the time and much appreciated. There have been many lessons learned over the course of a lifetime of fishing and one of them is to be respectful of each other's space and to mind your manners on the water because you never know when you might need a hand. The jerk who haunted Dan then insulted him believed there was no way for Dan to catch him or run into him but he was wrong. Dan told me that after their chance meeting he saw the interloper on two more occasions and when they spotted his boat they headed in the opposite direction. There are a few short cuts to success and one of them might be hiring a top notch charter skipper and learning from them. Hounding successful fishermen is not the way to go particularly if you run into someone who isn't reluctant to knock heads with you.

.

CLAM WARS

STANDING UP FOR YOUR RIGHTS

Up until then it was hard work, but seldom an impossible task to scratch up enough clams and quahogs when asked to fill a peck container of steamers for the old timers. It was a bright spring day when I pushed the heavy skiff off the Somerset shore after having considerably less success digging clams than I had been commissioned to excavate from that rocky shoreline. Due to the dismal economy, many of the men who would normally be working routine jobs had been laid off and were scratching fish and shellfish from the same shores to put on their tables or sell to the local taverns to pay for their nickel drafts. They were bigger and much stronger individuals who could turn over a huge swatch of shoreline on a low tide and they didn't leave much for a skinny kid with a bent clam rake. Those same rocky shores that had furnished me with buckets of clams and quahogs were all but picked clean, particularly those flats within walking distance of the residents of the heavily populated North End village.

I was looking forward to the steamers the old timer would prepare and I was not about to let him and my other mentors down, at least not if I could help it. It was still an hour from the bottom of the low tide so I allowed the strength of the outgoing current to carry the skiff while I stood up and prospected the shore; looking for a section that had not been worked over. I drifted under the Brightman Street Bridge and was dismayed to see two men already working the only productive section of bottom that gave up steamers, so I continued up the river and under the old Slades Ferry Bridge where I spotted yet another digger working the usually productive area in front of the towers. There was only one place left and it was a usually a dangerous option. The shoreline, from what we referred to as the point, was the last stretch of fertile rocky beach south of there to the old Somerset Shipyard. There were usually always good digging there but it was jealously guarded by some of the yards employees who regarded it as private property because they harvested their own shellfish there. I was told there was no such thing as private property along that low tide of our shoreline due to the old colonial fishing and fowling law but you couldn't convince that collection of combative workmen. A few months earlier one of the old gents from the club, who had fished

71

along that shore for decades, decided to dig a few quarts of clams to add to the white perch he had caught. He hauled his skiff up onto that contested rocky beach and began digging.

He claimed he had not so much as excavated half dozen clams when two men began shouting at him and making threats. A proud old Navy vet he looked up and presented them with the offending salute of the day then told them what he thought of their threats. That was when they sent out two men to harass him. He stood his ground using his pitch fork to fend them off but one of the men ran towards his skiff and pushed it off the beach where it drifted up into Mt Hope Bay. When he turned to rescue his boat the other man shoved him from behind and he hit the stones on his chest in a painful and awkward manner. When he finally got to his knees his boat had drifted out of reach and his assailants had stolen his digging tool and bucket. It was a long and painful walk back to the boat house and he was in pretty bad shape when he got there. A shot of home brewed White Lightning got his juices flowing and he recounted his story to the gathering. One of the young Turks that frequented the club was fresh out of the Marine Corps and ran to his car and headed for the shipyard hell bent and seeking retribution. The long walk home was what saved those bandits from a serious whipping because by the time the marine arrived at the shipyard gate it was locked up tight. From that point on the shipyard bullies led a charmed life. They found out from the watchman that they were being hunted by a muscular young man and they wanted no part of a fair fight, so both men, who lived in nearby Tiverton, Rhode Island began parking their car inside the fence before blasting out the gate at closing time.

It took a while but several weeks later after the heat was off, the brigands grew careless and one Friday afternoon flush with overtime pay they decided to visit the Sportsman's Café in the village to jump start their weekend. Unfortunately for them, once they began tipping too many boilermakers, the liquor began talking and they started bragging about their confrontation with the old Navy vet. Unbeknown to them, Anthony, a member of the boat house was sitting at a corner table and overhead them. He exited quietly to seek help and eventually located the marine who had been frustrated with his inability to settle the score for the treatment of his old friend. I would have given a bushel of hard won clams to have witnessed what transpired that evening, but if the numerous accounts about that confrontation were only half true those bullies got much more than they ever bargained for from a very angry leatherneck. Anthony said it began inside the bar when the marine challenged both men to step outside. Unwilling to expose them to a wide open melee they attempted to excuse themselves by saying the old man had started the fight. That was when the marine waded in and pasted the taller one dropping him with a single punch. He chased the other man, who ran outside, tackled him and administered a first class thumping. Old fashioned street justice had been served up in a swift and decisive manner.

Those thoughts were going through my mind as I drifted trying to gin up the courage to land the boat and dig in those forbidden grounds. The tide was about to turn so I chanced pulling the skiff up onto the prohibited beach and began digging with a sense of urgency. There was very little sign of digging in the rocky area where I beached so I rolled some soccer ball sized boulders aside and was rewarded with a few clams hiding under them right up on the surface. Between looking over my shoulder for danger and digging, I wore myself to a frazzle but I managed to harvest enough clams for our boil and headed home pulling hard on the oars and taking advantage of the incoming tide. I was torn between telling the old timers where I actually dug those clams because their concern for my safety had caused them to warn me away from there and after some deliberation I thought it would be better to keep those details to myself. For some reason that afternoons spicy boiled steamers extracted from illicit ground tasted much sweeter than any other. I learned a great deal about the ways of a successful waterman but the lessons on life were even more significant. I haven't dug a single clam along the shores of the Taunton River in decades, but I know where to look if I ever had to dig a few for bait. Today there are still a few stealthy old timers that harvest clams from those same areas. Some are closed because of pollution which is probably much less a factor today than back when everything was discharged directly into our rivers and bays. Whenever I see soft shell clams for sale I fondly recall the hard work that went into putting them on the counter and back to the clam wars of the old days when harvesting shellfish was more than just hard work, it was an adventure.

THE AUTHORS GRANDSON LLEYTON IS SCRATCHING CLAMS ALONG THE ROCKY SHORELINE OF MT HOPE BAY. THE DIGGING IS VERY DIFFICULT AND EACH AND EVERY CLAM IS HARD WON BUT ONCE THEY ARE STEAMED IN BEER AND SPICES IT IS WELL WORTH THE EFFORT.

HEAVY WEATHER BASS'N

WHY DO STRIPERS FEED MORE AGGRESSIVELY IN ROUGH WATER?

White water washed up the face of the steep black rock and licked at our heels. The tide was flooding and sooner than later we would have to evacuate our precarious perch or risk being washed off and dashed on the rocks below. It was the summer of 1960 and Russ and I were members of the Linesiders Bass Club and competing in the R. J. Schaeffer Saltwater Fishing Contest. We were fishing on the fabled Bull Rock, a misnomer for the huge boulder our competition named for the huge "bull" bass we hauled from that covert striper haunt. This story actually begins on a midsummer evening before we found that fabled rock while fishing a sandy section of beach along the craggy Little Compton shoreline. We had a 12 pound bass, three pounds short of the minimum Schaeffer contest weight requirements, lying on the sand and two huge scup that were able to get their mouths around the big hooks we twisted our fresh squid baits around. It was an hour before sunset when we first sighted the 16 foot outboard powered run-a-bout making its way toward white water cresting over a reef that is hidden just under the surface. The angler positioned his boat upwind of the structure and cast a large plug into the wash. From our vantage point we determined he was using heavy conventional gear and soon after the plug hit he reared back and set the hook on a large striper. We watched him fight the fish while backing the skiff away from the breaker by nudging the extended tiller with his knees. By the time the boat was positioned in deeper water away from the reef we watched him bend over the gunwale and gaff the fish in the jaw then slide the huge bass over the rail. We turned to each other in unison and uttered; "Did you see that?"

The skillful angler made two more passes and hooked up each time but only landed the last fish before his boat once again came dangerously close to reef. With his second fish in the boat he headed west and disappeared around the knob of the islands. We had attempted to fish the beachhead side of that structure but could seldom hold bottom, even with eight ounce sinkers because the force of the wash rolled and fouled our rigs, hanging them up on the gnarly bottom and causing us to lose most of our terminal tackle. That piece of bottom was always temptingly fishy but that night the mysterious angler convinced us that it was worth another try. What transpired next was to change our lives and the way we approached fishing. I realized the stripers didn't just appear on that reef they moved in from either side to take up station behind the structure to rest, hunt and ambush prey. We fished from numerous slippery perches until we settled on the aforementioned big rock because it afforded us a casting lane directly toward that reef yet far enough from the turmoil of roiling water to permit our offerings to remain in place. Bull Rock was a slippery glacial castoff on the that rugged shoreline, a location where five officially registered 50 pound stripers were captured along with dozens of bass in the 40-pound class all weighed on certified scales and entered in the R. J. Schaeffer Saltwater Fishing Contest. The vast majority of that class of fish were caught on bait in the form of fresh squid carefully wrapped around a gold 9/0 Eagle Claw hook and heaved out onto the perimeter of the reef some 65 yards distant.

Our tackle at the time was very basic. Russ and I used Penn Squidders filled with nine thread (27-pound test) J. D nylon line woven at a nearby Fall River spinning mill. The rods were the very early Lamiglass nine foot hollow glass blanks custom wound by Bridge Bait and Tackle a local landmark where we made most of our early tackle purchases. Terminal tackle was constructed from heavy linen leaders consisting of a single hook and a standard six or eight ounce bank sinker depending on the tidal conditions. I will leave the number and size of the broad shouldered stripers that broke our hearts and won their freedom to your imagination, but armed with that basic tackle and fishing the unforgiving boulder fields, our losses were numerous. We fished from that slippery perch for almost four years during which time we had tackle bags and bait stashes washed away and on one occasion I was washed off the rock in heavy weather while trying to gaff a 44-pound bass that Russ had hooked and which I was eventually able to jam my hand into its mouth and paddle my way to shore with. We hooked up with some enormous fish from that rock but we lost more than we landed until we formed a joint venture in which I purchased a boat and trailer and Russ provided the motor.

All during our partnership from the days in the surf, on the rock, then in the boat, it was the gusty southwest winds that always produced the best fishing. That usually coincided with the appearance of the mysterious fishermen who frequented this location on a regular basis. When it was calm he never seemed to catch but when there was whitewater he almost always landed fish. Although I grew up around boats and along the shore, the transition from the surf to the ocean was fraught with complications. The gnarly coastal area from Sakonnet Point, RI to Westport Harbor MA was a quantum leap from the waters of Mt Hope and Narragansett Bay; consequently we began our explorations with guarded optimism. It took a few years of alert and vigilant probing before we became comfortable in our new surroundings and during the time we moved from a 16 foot open plywood skiff to a classic Mackenzie Cuttyhunk, then onto a rugged 25 foot inboard powered McInnis bass boat. In the early years we dedicated most of our effort to casting large plugs into white water and subterranean structure and were liberally rewarded for our efforts. My favorite plugs were the inimitable Reverse Atom or stink plug, as one old timer deckmate called it because I loaded it up with crushed bunker gurry, the Atom B-40 surface swimmer and a bit later the giant jointed Creek Chub Pikes. Because of what some deckmates considered a character flaw I felt it was necessary to anoint all of my lures with natural scent, strong potions which they usually carried home on their shirts, pants and boots. I had statistics going for me because my side by side comparisons proved that scents worked.

Looking back on decades of outstanding trips one outing stands out for both our success and a close encounter with disaster. It had been a week of decent fishing until a storm produced gale force winds that gave the ocean a major stomach ache. Over the next two days the seas laid down but not enough to satisfy me. Russ was going fishing come hell or high water and the only reason I agreed to accompany him was because I was fearful he might catch a 50 and knock my 49 out of first place. The things I did for the sake of competition! The remnants of the heavy southwester had been rolling in all afternoon and by the time we made the turn at Sakonnet we could see white water washing up to the base of the breakwater beacon. This caused Russ to grin from ear to ear as conditions were right up his alley although I preferred fishing without taking a beating, but despite my protests my boyhood friend and longtime fishing partner had no intention of turning back. At that juncture of our careers we were outfitted with a pair of hard knocked Penn 704 spinning reels filled with Stren 30-pound test with 50-pound mono leaders taped onto medium-heavy eight foot custom spinning rods. After losing more fish than I care to admit because our large

77

brass snaps failed, even after crushing them closed, we switched to heavy a Duo-Lock snaps without further mishaps. While that tackle was adequate for most nearshore situations it was decidedly overmatched for what was in store for us that evening. I turned south at the breakwater and was greeted by a set of three white uppercuts that sent spray up and over the Cutty shield. I jogged into the steep waves until I could sneak between the lighthouse and the islands which afforded some protection and worked my way to the tip of East Island. Although it was rough the water was not as dirty as I anticipated and as we approached the first set of breakers there were a half dozen gulls rocking and rolling in a distinct slick of calmer water.

I put the boat abeam and Russ sent out his Reverse Atom. As I shifted into neutral I heard the magic words "fish on." Not bad for the first cast but it was to get much better. By the time we got his fish in the boat I had to move back up and take a cast while Russ kept our nose into the weather. My reverse hit the water and was immediately knocked in the air by a huge broom tailed bass. Two more strikes and misses due to the turbulent conditions caused the bass to have difficulty getting a purchase on the lure but they were certainly willing to pursue. One of several large linesiders in the chase finally grabbed the plug by the head and was rewarded with the bite of the sharp treble. Four jumbo bass were hauled from that reef but five more were lost before we moved off to another location that afforded us a bit more protection. It didn't seem to matter what structure we fished that evening as big stripers populated most of the locations but the seas were so chaotic it made it as difficult for them to grab the plugs as it did to retrieve them naturally, but finesse didn't seem to matter. With fish sliding about the cockpit it was difficult to maintain our balance and twice I slipped and fell on top of the motor box. Those few hours passed like a blur and just after sunset with 11 huge stripers sharing the slippery cockpit we took a breaker over the starboard quarter that nearly swamped us and I called it quits. Russ protested but not very persuasively. It was a long wet slog back to the harbor but once inside the protective granite barrier we hauled our catch up onto the dock and weighed them. Six of those bass were over 40 and the top two scaled 46 and 48 pounds. It was the biggest catch of jumbo stripers on plugs (a subsequent 1380 pound catch was made by casting live eels) either of us had ever experienced. Russ was right about heavy weather bass'n but as my mother was fond of saying, "be careful what you ask for?" That wild and wooly night was almost too much of a good thing!

These oldies but goodies were productive lures in their day and the author continues to employ them to capture trophy stripers. The Reverse Atoms and the Atom swimmers were productive lures particularly when they were immersed in herring or bunker gurry but the Russell lure and the Giant Pikes took more than their share of outsized stripers from the habitat that God created for striped bass.

HOMEWARD BOUND

THE AUTHOR HAS HAD HIS SHARE OF HAIRAISING ADVENTURES

The sharp forefoot of the sea kindly Downeaster bit into the shoulder of the wave and began its swift descent down across the face as up and down, side to side, we beat our way home. There was not an undertone of small talk or the good natured bantering that usually accompanies a successful fishing trip as we fought our way back to Cape Cod on a late winter day when the weather turned ugly. None of us had the stomach to look astern at the cresting following sea which hung over us like a bad dream. Someone observed that the waves looked higher than a three story building and no one on board challenged that premise. A 31-foot boat in a tranquil harbor surrounded by a fleet of run-a-bouts might appear impressive but in the teeth of that North Atlantic fury it was anything but. There were eight totes of steaker cod and two of smaller market cod lashed down to the deck, the result of four frantic hours of non-stop fishing. Our catch at the rate of that exceptional bite would have been much greater if not for the rapid change in the weather; it was almost as though the fish knew what was coming and went on a feeding binge. We left the harbor on a still March morning with the pre-dawn temperatures hovering around 30-degrees and the promise of a crisp but tranquil late winter day. The trip out to the ridges was uneventful as we busied ourselves with rigging and tackle preparation along with the good natured jousting that is prevalent in a cockpit heightened with expectation as we anticipated the first drop of the day.

No one strayed too far from the motor box and the heat escaping from the big diesel that was noisily propelling us to our offshore destination. To a man everyone rushed to the rail when the skipper cut back on the throttle and began searching for schools of fish or bait. He was in the process of adjusting the gain on the chart recorder when we heard the engine shift into reverse and felt that strong rearward surge. We gathered at the fish finder for a sight that would make the heart of any fisherman leap for joy. Rising up some 15-feet off the bottom was a large spike of bait with pods of much larger targets all around it. We had arrived at Little Georges. I don't believe I drew a single breath as my jig fell through the depths on the way to the bottom. There was no conversation at that point as everyone was determined on putting the all important first fish in the box. We had arrived as planned at slack water and my nine ounce Zing jig made it to the bottom before the heavier Norwegian iron clams, my companions were fishing, dropped into the strike zone. After two turns of the handle I felt that wonderful surge of a fish heading in the opposite direction. It was a deep drop and way too many turns on the handle of that low ratio reel before we saw the white belly of the fish in the cold clear waters below. That cod broke the surface, hooked fair in the top of the jaw, as I declined the gaff, lifting the five-pounder up and over the rail and directly into a tote.

The bite was as fast and furious; much more than any of us had anticipated with hookups as soon as we could get the jig down but the skipper was unhappy with the size of these fish as he was looking for steaker codfish over the 25-pound mark; the size and numbers he had located two days prior, and not the five to eight pound cod were holding over. Over the years I've left this type of bite to move off prospecting for bigger fish and I always execute these moves with great trepidation. Several miles and numerous drops later I hooked a fish that took me back down and would not give up the bottom. We had finally located the steakers. Over the next few hours we hooked and lost an enormous amount of fish in the 25 to 40-pound class until I felt an uncomfortable sensation creeping up the back of my exposed neck. The skipper had been fishing close to the helm in the protection of the pilot house on the downwind side of the boat and did not notice the subtle wind shift until I brought it to his attention. The VHF had been crackling all morning long bringing us the gossip, tall tales and colorful language of the dragger fleet located much farther out on the bank. A few minutes after my warning one of the draggers skippers called out to no one in particular that, "we've got some weather coming." It was all downhill from then on.

It's difficult to leave the quality of fish and the intensity of the bite we were over that day and a couple of my deckmates looked puzzled when the skipper gave the order to haul back quickly and pack everything in. I secured all the totes and loose gear to the cleats as we turned and began the long steam home. Less than 45 minutes after we pulled up stakes the two anglers who were sulking because we left those fish so abruptly were wide-eyed and pale faced at just how unexpectedly that weather turned ugly. Over a lifetime of fishing and boating that trip ranks right up there as one of the most perilous and menacing I have ever been on. All it would have taken was an engine malfunction of any sort, a fuel contamination problem due to the violent tossing of the hull, or one mistake by the skipper and we would have been added to a long list of maritime statistics. As you may have theorized by this time we made it back safely with a great deal of credit to our skipper and that sturdy seaworthy hull which rode those violent seas the way her designer and builder had intended. Any offshore trip should be thoughtfully and thoroughly planned and prepared for long before you slip the dock lines. If there is any question at all about weather or the capability of the craft you will be sailing on you should reconsider and look to alternatives. The painful fact is that fishing beyond the sight of land in the warmer months can be risky while fishing in March and the fickle transitional colder months are usually a very dangerous proposition. Although many of the small boat owners I speak with are raring to go many of them are far from ready to cope with the vagaries of anything but ideal fair weather conditions. Experience may seem an expensive commodity but under difficult conditions you will find it's worth every dollar it costs to acquire.

AUTHOR'S NOTE: Some fishermen never learn and unfortunately I'm one of them. Over a long, and less than illustrious fishing career, I could fill a few chapters in this book about bad decisions and close calls. The aforementioned trip should have provided enough offshore adventures to last a lifetime but it didn't. A few years later in response to a call from a friend in need I sailed offshore on another ill fated cod trip which I documented in the November issue of On The Water Magazine. I only hope that was my last such encounter of the frightening variety.

GREAT EATING FISH BUT WOULD YOU RISK YOUR LIFE FOR ONE?

SNAPPING CLAWS AND LOBSTER WARS

DON'T MESS WITH A LOBSTER POT UNLESS YOU HAVE A DEATH WISH

It was a white knuckle trip across a slick calm Buzzards Bay, one I wouldn't have normally made in fog this thick but the squalls of the previous two days prevented us from hauling our lobster pots and it was our duty to tend them. My son Peter sat up forward on the top of the cuddy cabin watching intently for any wake or ripple that would indicate the presence of another vessel in the area. His keen ears were isolated from the sound of the big outboard churning up a slight wake at a modest 2000 RPM's as he strained to locate the direction of the foghorns of other craft making their passage through the main commercial thoroughfare of the bay. The trip which would have taken 25-minutes under normal early morning conditions consumed well over an hour but the Loran-C coordinates of the northernmost pot buoy my son had plugged into that reliable nav aide put us right on the mark. Our lookout spotted the tall black and white striped stick protruding from the Marconi buoy waving in the tide and pointed in that direction. I'd made my share of compass and pocket watch runs across this area of busy marine traffic and was always relieved to arrive at the entrance to Quicks and Robinsons Hole but I doubt I would ever have been able to find that needle in the haystack without that remarkable Sitex navigation machine.

My lookout scurried back into the cockpit, slipped on his yellow apron and grabbed the boat hook as I steered us up to the pot. The buoy was dumped on the cockpit deck while the pot line was slipped into the roller sheave of the pot hauler as the boy began the arduous task of lifting a water soaked oaken pot up from 55-feet of water. Just as the pot broke the surface we could hear the rewarding sounds of lobster tails clacking; a sound that still brings a smile to my face up to this very day. With the pot on the gunwale Peter opened the lid and removed the old bait bag before sticking his gloved hand in to grasp the largest lobster. The big bug waved its crusher claw in defiance but a deft hand moved around and grasped it by the body. The big lobster had made short work of the other two crustaceans in the pot that took refuge in the corners of the trap; their broken claws strewn about the oak lathes. The lobster gauge confirmed the largest lobster was at least two pounds while another was just over the legal limit. The legal cull would be tossed in a spiced brew and become a portion of our evening meal. The other lobster's body carapace was just short of the legal minimum and was tossed back where it would grow new claws (they are able to grow them slowly) and live to feed and fight another day.

From the perspective of the tourist or the occasional boater lobstering looks like fun and it can be, for the first few days or weeks of a long season. From the time I began hauling eel pots with Taunton River watermen every pot marker buoy was a ribbon on a Christmas present about to be opened. Depending on who I crewed for that day we usually began hauling pots at or before first light and ran up one side of the river and down the other shore hauling, what were usually small cork float markers that would not engender as much attention as a Clorox bottle or some type of bright buoy that would attract the river pirates. I loved hauling traps and although it was demanding physical work I couldn't wait to roll the pots over the gunwale to see what our bait had attracted. Besides the meat eels (all the specimens of the size we now refer to as bass eels were released to grow another season) we caught green crabs, small blueshells, toadfish and occasionally choggies and small white perch which squeezed their way into the narrow traps funnel. Because he knew and shared my anticipation my tutor allowed me to haul the first several pots until my young arms tired then my job was to sort the eels by size and toss back the whips and shorts. We had good days, great days and the stormy days when some night pirate hit the trap line. Those thieves of the lowest order would not only empty the pots and steal the contents but they would occasionally pilfer the pots and set them in another location.

Whenever Leo hauled a pot and his neck and face turned a beet red I knew we were in trouble. Some of those eel pots were so loaded they bent under the weight of the eels as we hauled them to the surface so when he pulled on a line and felt very little resistance he knew someone had been tampering with his gear. It didn't matter if we caught a record number of eels in a single day because if someone had pulled or stolen one of his traps it was an injury to his psyche and he dwelt on the negative rather than the first-rate catch. I was to experience that the same feeling was contagious when I began setting lobster pots when my pilot cabin Parker 25 was moored in Padanaram harbor. A typical day consisted of setting out of South Dartmouth before dawn and arriving at the first pot at sunrise. Peter and I hauled pots while his mother kept a log book of our progress including pot numbers, locations and the number of keepers and shorts we discarded as well as the number of protected eggers (female lobsters with an egg mass under their bodies) we carefully returned to spawn. We were setting our gear on a wreck site I had discovered while we were doing research for our book Fishable Wrecks and Rockpiles. The wreck had been on the sea bottom for quite some time and offered protection for small bait fish and their natural predators as well as lobsters and crabs. It was a very productive location and I don't recall a single day when we didn't have more than enough lobster for our table, family and friends.

That was before the pilferage started. One warm August day the first three pots we pulled were not only empty the thieves made no effort to hide their transgressions leaving the trap door open when they tossed the pot back. As you might imagine this type of behavior is capable of eliciting very strong feelings of retaliation however if you are the type of individual who turns their cheek to every insult or blow then you wouldn't understand or approve of my retort. I won't burden you with the details of my reaction to being pirated other than to say that I conspired with two other lobstermen from the same harbor where we determined the thieves were situated as they were also being raided. After our reprisal I can assure you the burglars were never seen in our potting area again and I doubt if they ever pulled another lobster pot that didn't belong to them. Lobstermen are usually very independent and hardworking individuals who set and tend their traps in all sorts of weather and all they ask is to be allowed to haul their gear without interference. The lobstermen (and there are a few short-sighted individuals) who keep and sell undersized lobster (shorts) are the ones who are killing the very resource that feeds them.

My advice to any fishermen or boat operator who plies the waters where lobster pots are set is to give them a wide berth and be extremely careful about long lengths of floating line on the surface that can foul a prop and disable or even sink a boat. The life of a lobsterman is not as carefree as the casual observer might guess. Men have been beaten senseless, shot at and had their boats sunk at their moorings over disagreements and territorial disputes about lobster fishing which to this day stirs a heightened passion in those individuals who participate in this traditional method of fishing. The next time you enjoy a lobster dinner, lobster roll or a delicious lobster salad take a moment to thank the men and women who worked so hard to put that delicacy on your table.

LOBSTERING IS HARD WORK PARTICULARLY IF YOU ARE HAULING BY HAND. DON'T MESS WITH ANYONE'S LOBSTER GEAR UNLESS YOU HAVE A DEATH WISH.

.

RIDING OUT A STORM

USING YOUR SENSES TO AVOID DANGEROUS WEATHER

The first sounds of danger came in the form of muffled booms from way off in the distance. With a cobalt blue sky and high thin white clouds under a dazzling sun conditions suggested I had all the ingredients for a great early summer day. Looking to the west the visibility was well over 20-miles with a slight haze but the forecasters had called for the possibility of a thunder shower, much the same as they do just about every summer day when there is bright sun, colder air in the upper atmosphere, and high humidity. The fact is that if I were to allow those "potential" forecasts to keep me off the water there would be very little fishing done during the course of the summer. I am not suggesting that you ignore the weather forecasts, quite the contrary. You should obtain a daily forecast the night before any fishing or boating trip then monitor the weather on your marine radio weather band all day long. I can't stand the constant chatter of the marine VHF radio because what is being launched over the airways is primarily mindless and needless chatter until some kids gets their hands on the mike. That is when any semblance of protocol and the intended use of this valuable resource head straight for the dumpster.

The weather channel can be monitored hourly if conditions in your immediate area appear changeable. Most of the summer afternoon storms in our area come out of the north-north west which is where the thunderstorms roar along the ocean front and up the major waterways such as Narragansett Bay, the east and west passages and the Sakonnet River. I have been caught out in two very serious storms, both of which were not predicted. The first occurred in Vineyard Sound where we were fishing off Tarpaulin Cove and catching jumbo sea bass on nearly flat calm seas. With my marine background and the education I received from some of the best seamen in the area I always keep a visual check on the weather. While we can't see wind or temperature changes we certainly can feel them however clouds are a great visual aid to changing weather. On this particular day it was about 1:30 PM when I felt a slight westerly breeze on the back of my neck and turned to see a few low dark clouds forming in the direction of Block Island.

My vigilance meter ascended and I began fishing and looking west rather than towards Woods Hole.

Our marine weather band (this was long before Doppler Weather Radar) continued with the same forecast it has been broadcasting since sunrise but what I was seeing was the formation of a storm over the ocean as the low lying clouds were gathering moisture and becoming darker with every passing minute. I called for all lines to be hauled which was not very a very popular pronouncement however I insisted and started the engine and began heading for Robinson's Hole. When I first saw that cloud it was at least 20 miles distant but before I was able to travel less than six miles that thick gray thunderhead was right on top of us causing calm seas to crest and, during the last mile in our dash for safety, we were pounding our way over three to five foots seas that were building. We made the shelter of Robinsons where I set the anchor and grimaced as lightning bolts struck the island and the water all around us. My wife and son were visibly shaken and I was worried because it was my responsibility to protect them and get them home safely. We spent over two hours in the lee with thunder, lightning and driving rain so strong that it exploded on the surface causing water to burst and shoot upwards. Those were two of the longest hours I can remember.

Once the storm passed the sun broke through and a huge rainbow bridged the sound from the Elizabeth Islands to the Vineyard as we rode home over Buzzards Bay in relatively calm seas. This past Tuesday I fished off Newport under ideal conditions with a mild south wind and sunny to overcast conditions caused by a thickening mass of the heavy cloud cover. Once again the forecast had called for the possibility of thunderstorms so I kept a weather eye out toward the west. Sometime around 1:30 PM low clouds could be seen west of Jamestown at which time I turned on the marine weather band. It was then I heard the grating horn that warns of a dangerous weather system. The thunderstorm I was watching was passing offshore to the south but unbeknownst to me there was also one cutting across Aquidneck Island and heading west. I was now caught between two systems so I tucked in behind a high bluff off Ocean Drive, put on my foul weather gear and waited for the storms to pass. It was then that the marine band predicted dangerous thunder heads with hail and lightning with wind gusts up to 60-miles per hour. I seldom run the boat at speeds in excess of 20-knots and then only for a short period of time but being sandwiched between two storm fronts of this magnitude was something I didn't relish so I pushed the reliable E-Techs throttle to the firewall and steamed across the building seas of the Sakonnet River and headed for sanctuary of the harbor. That was when I saw the second front between Fogland and Portsmouth and watched the thick gray mass that was so low it appeared to be sitting on the water. Lightning strikes illuminated the dark sky as the heavy rain and hail caught up to me as I pulled into the harbor.

With the large sailboats at the entrance to the harbor and the larger lobster and gill net boats I felt somewhat relieved that I was no longer the high point on the water and a target for a lightning bolt. After twenty minutes of rain, wind, hail and sleet the sun appeared and the gusts dropped off to a gentle breeze. After waiting an additional 20 minutes I headed back out over the nearly slick surface but before I reached my destination the marine band sounded yet another alert. Looking north up the Sakonnet River another thunderhead was forming. So far I'd been betting on the weather changing and it did-only it was for the worse. After all these years on the water this was the very first time I had ever been caught out in more than one major storm which in this case numbered three. I learned a lesson that afternoon and that was never to take storms for granted or to lump them into a group but consider them as separate entities. Being caught out in three storms is two storms too many for me.

From midsummer on we are entering a period of unsettled weather right up to late August and early September when the very real threat of hurricanes is added to the mix. Never take weather for granted. Listen to the forecast, keep your VHF marine radio tuned to the weather band and during the early to late afternoons keep an eye on the western horizon. Today's weather forecasts are quite sophisticated and a quantum leap from the days of the 1938 hurricane that took everyone by surprise. There are enough hazards on the water but if we keep a "weather eye" surprise storms don't have to be one of them.

CHAPTER IV

CLOSE ENCOUNTERS OF THE FIRST ORDER

FISHING WITH A KNOWLEGABLE SKIPPER CAN PAY BIG DIVIDENDS

CHARTERING DURING THE GOLDEN ERA OF STRIPED BASS FISHING

IT WILL COST YOU MORE THAN SIXTY BUCKS TODAY BUT HOOKING UP WITH AN EXPERIENCED SKIPPER WILL USUALLY PAY BIG DIVIDENDS

Today you might consider it inexpensive but trying to scrape together fifty dollars for a charter trip during the late 50's was no easy feat. I am not talking about just any charter trip but an outing with the best of the best. Would you be interested in participating in a striped bass charter at Cuttyhunk with one of the best fishermen on the east coast? I thought so! Back in the 1960's Charlie Cinto and his pal Russ Keene chartered Captain Frank Sabatowski of the June Bug and Charlie Haag of the Strad. Cinto and Haag charged the princely sum of $50 for a trip and the arrangement for these two seasonal regulars with both skippers was sharing in half of the catch. Even with stripers selling for meager 25 cents a pound there were many a trip that the customers ended up with a free trip and change to spare, something that occasionally annoyed the hard working skippers. Well aware that they were getting preferential treatment Cinto and his friend always saw to it that the captain received the lion's share of the purse which kept their seats (maple kitchen chairs with sawed off legs) secure throughout what many regard as the Golden Era of striped bass fishing. Another Cuttyhunk charter regular was Jay Vee a member of my Fall River Linesiders Bass Club who fished with those high liners and not a season passed without him either scoring a 50 or a high 40-pound fish. His October 55 pound striper aboard Captain Bob Smith's Susan B knocked my Newport ocean drive 53 out of first place.

For those who could not afford what was to us an expensive proposition Cinto points out that many workmen were barely earning $3.00 dollars an hour. A few of the senior members of the Weetamoe Yacht Club would gang up to take day trips on lobster boats to bottom fish in the Woods Hole or Vineyard Sound area where one or sometimes two bushel bags of scup or sea bass were typical for an all day trip which cost about $5.00 a head. My friend Russ Malone split a four man Cuttyhunk charter (about $ 15 bucks a man) on a boat called the Beagle. Despite rough conditions Russ caught two fish over 40-pounds and became hooked on Cuttyhunk fishing. Today a six pack (six man) charter on a bass boat will run you anywhere from $450 up to $675 or more depending on how far that skipper travels to the bass grounds. As in everything else you get what you pay for because there are "paper" captains out there who passed the Coast Guard test but do not have the experience or the expertise to charge those fees. I fully realize that in order to gain experience you have to develop it but paying for someone's fuel and education is not my idea of how to go about arranging for a successful charter. The old fashioned way was to mate for a captain or captains to accumulate your days at sea which would serve you well in your intended career. If you find a charter fee that sounds a bit too inexpensive there is usually a reason. There are quite a few experienced charter skippers who paid their dues with decades of service on the water so if you don't know anyone who has fished with them ask them for references which any good skipper should be happy to provide. Today there are numerous pamphlets in local bait and tackle shops advertising the services of area skippers. If you need help in making a decision ask the shop owner or a knowledgeable clerk who should steer you in the right direction. Of course it would be impossible to guarantee success on every single trip but you can usually determine in short order if the skipper is capable and if he is giving it his all to produce fish for you.

Back in the days of extreme corporate generosity there was a big name association fund raiser that dedicated its summer activity to striped bass fishing. For those members who owned sizable boats but didn't possess fishing expertise the group hired local fishermen with proficiency in the capture of the seven striped fish. One of the association's officers was a client of mine who recommended me for this lucrative assignment. The first two years I skippered the boat of a wealthy corporate type who was only interested in putting bloody fish on his deck as long as it didn't interfere with the partying. His boat was so big (just under mega yacht status-my boat is bigger than your boat) that I could not put us in close to the areas where stripers were in residence so I opted to fish deeper water which regardless of the wind and tide was usually accompanied with swells. By the time I located a sizable pod of stripers two members of the crew who were liberally plied with a potent green melon libation began puking $50 lunches over the rail. The first year we had fish in the 20-pound class that never made it to the scales on time because I obtained permission to mercifully dock the boat in a nearby harbor so the ailing crew members could regain their sea legs and quiet their heaving stomachs. The next two years of rocking and rolling in top heavy yachts I asked for a demotion to a bass boat, hopefully something under 26-feet however fully aware that size craft does not accommodate a stateroom and salon along with full bar and numerous other amenities. I did get downgraded to 31-foot sports fishermen that had seen much better days along with a captain whose face would have cracked if God forbid he ever attempted to smile.

I choked back my initial response and mated for the company dignitaries which consisted of a group of four women out fishing for the very first time. They paid for the charter and my fee but my inside connection, who was aware of my propensity for candid observations, asked me to keep my opinions and comments to a minimum and not step on the skippers toes. I made the guests as comfortable as possible on this old battlewagon but the tackle was old and in poor repair and it was evident from the outset when the captain put out two wire lines outfits with huge tubes without a trace of worm or teaser that he was only interested in getting this job over with because he would never see these people again. We trolled for two hours without so much as a sniff when I went up to the bridge and politely asked if he would mind if I rigged his lines with my own tubes and some fresh worms I had covertly brought aboard. He took a long drag on his smoke, shot me a disgusted look and said, "Knock yourself out." First of all I know it's difficult if not impossible to assist a charter patron while you are eight to ten feet up on the flying bridge. That is why you can't beat the intimacy of a bass boat where the skipper is working the cockpit right alongside you. I cut his worn leaders, replaced them with new Berkley leader material and tied on my rigs. In less than 15 minutes, trolling over the same bottom both rods were doubled over with bluefish. The captain looked astern and just kept on moving. Amid screams of fear and joy we managed to boat two bloody blues in the five pound class and when they hit the deck all four woman displayed their athleticism by jumping atop the big Igloo coolers alongside each rail.

I swear to you there was not a single word of acknowledgement or encouragement from a now ticked off skipper that I tried my best not to upstage. We were both being adequately compensated to insure that these ladies had an enjoyable trip but I was the only one holding up my end of the bargain. We ended that wearisome trip with the ladies boating nine bluefish and two small stripers that were released. At the end of the day I snipped off my tubes and was about to carry the catch off the boat when the skipper asked if they would like him to fillet their catch. I had noticed two very dull and rusted knives in a rack inside the companionway so I volunteered to clean them back at the marina. Even though those intelligent and generous women had never been on a fishing trip before they were well aware of the captain's deficiency and not one of them offered to tip him. On the other hand after I had cleaned and iced their catch they rewarded me with a gourmet dinner at a harbor side restaurant and when I opened my knife roll the following day there were five crisp twenties tucked in the pocket. When you strive to provide your very best most people know how to say thank you.

THERE WILL BE BLOOD

WITH HOOKS, GAFFS AND KNIVES-YOU WILL EVENTUALLY BLEED

You won't believe me and you would probably have good cause not to. Anyone who has been fishing as long as I have and claims to have never been bitten by a live bluefish is probably a braggart or a liar; or maybe a little bit of both. But with over 50 years of handling the nasty yellow eyed chopping machines my flesh had never been penetrated by the razor sharp teeth of a live bluefish. Oh, I've been slashed by blues but only when I have been careless while lifting them from the fish box or removing their flesh on the cutting board. That was the unblemished truth until August 17th, 2012 at exactly 12:20 PM while fishing off Westport's Elephant Rock Beach. My friends, Dana Norman and Jimmy Figuredo, were trolling my tubes and feeding a host of voracious blues in the three to five pound class that were hell bent on putting us out of the sea worm trolling business. The toothy critters were slashing the jumbo sea worms as fast as we could put them on the hook while others were intent on taking a toll on the tough vinyl tubes that presented the tempting crawlers. Most of the smaller blues were allowed to escape boat side as we held onto the tubes while they performed their acrobatics and finally spit the hook. We were looking for a few husky stripers to steak for the cookout at the client's house in Rhode Island later that evening but after five hours all we were able to scratch up were five stripers from 27 to 34 inches a size that would not do justice to the labor intensive process of the steaking routine.

We moved off the rocks along that beach and headed for the deeper and hopefully more productive holes off that point of land. As luck would have it the grandparents of the bluefish we left were waiting for us and one was big enough to fool us into thinking we had finally hooked up with a 30-pound bass. When the jumbo blue came alongside I noticed the hook was deep and into the gill area and the fish was bleeding profusely. That one was not a candidate for a live release so I gaffed it and brought it into the boat. The only safe way to handle a bluefish, if there is such a way, is to grasp them firmly behind the head with a thumb and finger pressed into the recesses of the gills. That way if the fish struggles violently you can merely release your grip and the fish will fall on the deck or into a fish box. That is a strategy that has worked for me time and again up until the aforementioned date and time. That fish was not going to go quietly into the fish box so I held it over the big Igloo cooler and as I began to release my grip the fish turned and raked its wicked sharp teeth right across my right thumb. Blood spurted from the wound and no one was more surprised than me to see the damage those teeth had inflicted. I usually purchase ten packs of face cloths to use as rags and always have one in my pocket or nearby to mop up spills or wipe my hands so I immediately pulled the towel from my back pocket and covered up the wound while Dana went hunting for the first aid kit.

Before he located the Band-Aids I had almost completely blood soaked the cloth and was looking for another one to cut into strips to bind the wound and stop the bleeding because a Band-Aid was not going to impede the flow. It only stands to reason that the first slash from a live bluefish was going to be a significant episode because I had not seen that kind of bloodletting since I ripped the jugular on a bass I was preparing for steaking. I went through two more cloths before the wound began to close and we were finally able to put two Band-Aids on it but the cut to my thumb interfered with my line handling and filleting duties for the remainder of that trip. I have relived that bite over and over again and I still can't understand how that fish was able to turn and bite me when I had a secure grip from behind its menacing teeth. There are numerous tales about bluefish biting incidents, most of them exaggerated but their piranha like teeth can and do inflict serious harm. Horror stories the likes of the one I am about to relate have been taken to extremes but one of my surf fishing buddies from the Cape told me about an incident on Nauset Beach over 25 years ago that makes me very uncomfortable every time I think about it. Rich is a high-line surf fisherman who had guided anglers on the Cape beaches for decades and this particular night he had an enthusiastic 20-year old, new to surf fishing in New England waters in his charge. After moving to several locations they found a large school of feeding stripers just at dusk but the fish would not take plugs so they set up sand spikes and began catching bass in the 18 to 22-pound class on sea worms and bait floats. After showing the young man how to remove the hooks and toss the bass up on the beach away from the tide line they moved about 25 yards apart.

About 20 minutes later Rich described what came from down the beach as a blood curdling scream. He raced over thinking the kid had stuck a sharp 7/0 hook in his hand only to find the boy's right hand covered in blood. There was only one bluefish along that entire beach that night and the boy hooked it. In the dark he stuck his hand up inside the mouth of the fish and was rewarded with a painful bite. Rather than wait for the fish to open its mouth he pulled his arm out and ripped the skin from both sides of his hand. Rich had illuminated the area with his bright headlamp and knew he had to get the kit to the hospital in a hurry. He gathered up their rods but left his sand spikes and fish strewn all over the sand as he made his way off the beach to the emergency room. They called the resident surgeon down to have a look at it and thankfully he was an old hand at removing fish hooks and stitching up cuts, however, these wounds would require a bit more time than that. The doctor sent Rich back to the beach to recover his gear and upon his arrival he found his sand spikes and their catch of fish in a big igloo cooler. There was a note from one of his friends with instructions to meet up with him at the Gorilla Hole (a deep pocket near Nauset Inlet) when he was able. Who said there were no Good Samaritans left? My grateful friend loaded the fish and gear into his beach buggy then drove to the point to meet his buddies. This was in the era long before cell phones and when he conveyed the story his friend, even that hardened old surf jockey who had seen just about everything, grimaced. Back at the emergency room my friend recovered the victim who had been given antibiotic injections and had his hand wrapped in soft bandages right up to his wrist. For all he had been through he was in good humor and told Rich he couldn't wait to hit the beach again, only this time with a good headlight so he could properly identify the nature of his catch.

When we come right down to it the great sport of fishing is froth with dangers. We fish from beaches with deep drop-offs, fish from boats among dangerous rips and reefs and cast lures and baits adorned with sharp hooks. We land fish with pointed gaffs then handle specimens with long sharp spines. Over the years I've made a few visits to the emergency room for serious puncture wounds when large striper dorsal fins penetrated my boots and caused painful infections. All that considered it is the devil bluefish that is the bloodletting antagonist of the highest order. During my decades of fishing I've seen some pretty nasty cuts inflicted by bluefish, one where a good sized chopper had bitten down on a little finger right to the bone. Remember a bluefish has incredible eyesight and they never stop moving. If you have one bouncing around on the deck don't reach down to try and pick it up. If there is the slightest bit of life left in him old yellow eye will detect that movement and go right after anything that gets close to it including metal pliers and knives and they are often reluctant to give up their prizes. Remember that when bluefish are in residence fishermen have much more than an errant hook to worry about.

A GAFF HOOK HAS A MURDEROUS POINT. TURN YOUR MOUNTED GAFF HOOKS INWARD SO CREW MEMBERS CANNOT WALK INTO THEM.

LUCK TAKES A HOLIDAY

CONFESSIONS OF A REPLACEMENT ANGLER ON A CUTTYHUNK STRIPER TRIP

"I smell bass" at least that's what I thought he said. I looked upwards from my uncomfortable position as he repeated his declaration. We had been dulled by the cold wet dampness and the complete lack of action. Never look a gift horse in the mouth my father warned me, however, on this night I believed I did and the horse bit me in the face. I had no business being there, sitting on this severed leg maple kitchen chair on the deck of this seakindly Brownell bass boat yet here I was. I believed that God had not only listened to my prayers but he had granted me an oft wished request to be fishing on a charter boat at Cuttyhunk. Back in the early Cuttyhunk days only the sports, a few bankers, insurance executives and a cadre of hard working self employed individuals could afford a charter trip to the island of many stones.

Charlie Cinto was a working stiff who logged numerous overtime hours and worked a part time job in order to pay for his fishing habit. He told me that back in the 1960's he and his pal Russ Keane paid the princely sum of $50.00 per trip with Captain Frank Sabatowski with negotiations allowing for a split of the proceeds of the catch with the skipper. Even at the going rate of $ .25 to .30 cents a pound for stripers at that time on most occasions the men earned a free trip and some folding money to boot. Not bad for a couple of blue collar guys satisfying their striper habit. I made it to the big time with a little bit of luck-both the good and the bad kind. The man who had booked the trip with my deckmate was given a choice. Stay at home and attend a family memorial service or go fishing and face the prospect of divorce. It was a no brainer. The family man stayed at home and his partner was not able to sell his spot at the last minute so the poor kid from the north end got to make his first charter fishing trip to Cuttyhunk. That is how this dream trip turned out to be a nightmare. We trolled Sow and Pigs without so much as a tap before slogging our way over to the Vineyard to fish the rip at Gay Head. We arrived cold, wet and thoroughly beaten after lifting our hoods in a vain attempt to keep the cold salt spray off our aching bodies. Devils Bridge was no less productive and after two hours of crawling up then sliding down frothy waves we headed back to the south side of Nashawena where we trolled swimming plugs to the monotonous drone of the reliable Crusader Marine engine. I began to think that the other guy must have had a premonition of this nightmare trip and backed out while feigning a family emergency.

I had shriveled up into my damp foul weather gear and was somewhere between exhaustion and boredom when the captain announced that he smelled bass. The only thing I'd smelled was the noxious engine exhaust when we were trolling downwind so by the time he made the second declaration I was still a bit groggy. Not 30-seconds after he scented fish our rods bent under the strain of hefty stripers. It took almost six hours of pain and misery but it was well worth it. We came alive as fish slammed big plugs and the skipper gaffed and rolled them over the gunwale. After two hours of lock and load fishing we were standing on a deck littered with big stripers. My deckmate recorded a 44-pound fish while I caught my personal best at that time which was a fat 38-pound specimen. After two hours of that frantic fishing flurry I was so wired I wouldn't have been able to sleep, not even in my own warm bed. That activity went a long way toward restoring my energy level not to mention my body core temperature. On the way back to Fairhaven the skipper had the rear tiller stuck in his backside while his teeth clenched down on the stub of a soggy cigar. My benefactor slept while I looked out over the wide expanse of Buzzards Bay as the first traces of a new day broke in the east. After the boat was secured in its slip we unloaded the fish into the skipper's pickup truck and he was off to New Bedford to sell the catch.

It would have been nice to stop for hot coffee and a satisfying breakfast but both of us had to rush home to shower and get dressed for a full day of work. On the drive back to my home in Fall River my sponsor suggested that I keep the outcome of the trip low key so as not to antagonize or rub it in the nose of the man whose spot I took. The person I was a stand-in for was never informed that he missed one of the best trips of his life because it would have served no purpose other than to cause him anguish. My partner informed me that he told the man it was a tough trip where we scratched several locations to put together a catch and he was satisfied. On their next trip with the same Cuttyhunk Hi-Line skipper they fished on the celebrated June moon and only caught two small stripers and one bluefish but that's why they call it fishin' and not catchin'. The renowned Cuttyhunk skippers and their seaworthy bass boats plied Sow and Pigs from mid May through mid October with a success rate that was the envy of all the other east coast striper ports. Those were the days when Charlie Tilton would sit in the rocking chair on his front porch and hold court for an admiring audience. I was one of the very fortunate minions who would visit the 86-year old skipper, who at the time was the oldest active licensed guide in the entire country, and soak up his words of wisdom. There was a great deal of competition and in many instances animosity between the charter skippers who were all vying for the top spot on the leader board and their share of the well-heeled patrons.

I can recall when Lloyd Bosworth, Charlie Smith, Charlie Haig and Frank Sabatowski were booked solid one year in advance and if you wanted to fish the preferred dates around the June full moon you might have to book two years in advance and pay a $ 25.00 premium, which was a good chunk of change during an era when all night fares with tackle including round trip from New Bedford to the islands were going for $ 60.00. That was the one and only charter trip I ever made to Cuttyhunk but it was something to remember and learn from. After that trip it was my privilege to have market fished with Captain Frank Sabatowski when he didn't have a paying customer or perhaps had a cancellation that he could not fill at the last minute. I also fished with my dear friend and mentor Captain Roland Coulombe in his Bristol, Sakonnet and Dyer bass boats making the long trip from his Somerset Motel to Cuttyhunk, many times back and forth on the same day. On one trip Coulombe and me caught 26 stripers in the 20-pound class (quite a feat for a mid spring outing) on May 18th then returned to the exact same spot the following day and fished the same lures without so much as a promise.

At that time of year the fish were migrating toward the Cape and the school we picked those fish from might have been swimming past Woods Hole by the time we hit that location again. Was the May 18th catch all luck? I certainly don't believe it was. We were out scouting for fish that week so we deserved the reward unlike some other fishermen who might have happened on the scene and got lucky to have run into fish on their first trip of the season. Despite my views and the opposing ideology of other fisherman there will always be an issue as to what constitutes the difference between luck and skill although we all can be certain that the result is fantastic fishing when we experience a combination of the two.

THIS 1964 PHOTO OF HOWARD VICKERY, RUSS KEANE AND CAPTAIN CHARLIE HAAG WAS TAKEN BY CHARLIE CINTO UPON THEIR RETURN TO NEW BEDFORD FROM CUTTYHUNK. HOW MANY 50'S DO YOU COUNT AND WOULD YOU SPEND $60 FOR A TRIP LIKE THIS? PHOTO BY CHARLIE CINTO

FLY FISHING

THE HUMBLE BEGINNINGS OF A NON TRADITIONAL FLY RODDER

Am I a fly fisherman? Not hardly; at least not by today's gentlemanly fly fishing standards. Fifty years ago we used fly rods, and crude hand tied streamers to deceive small, medium and whenever we won the white knuckle battles of the pilings, a jumbo striper for our efforts. We didn't employ fly fishing gear for sporting reasons because we were market fishing, but the financial reward didn't dampen our enthusiasm for the long wand nor the thrills or the experience of fooling bass with fish feathers and bucktails. On numerous occasions the fly rod was the weapon of choice dictated by conditions because all of the above undertakings began quite innocently and accidentally. We were fishing the old Slades Ferry railroad bridge, a two story draw bridge which spanned the Taunton River just shy of the junction where that river meets Mt Hope Bay. Initially the method of choice was a homemade bucktail jig spiced with a piece of sea worm and normally cast up tide and worked back towards the shadows alongside the structure. When the fish were there the hits usually came when the lure was almost straight up and down or just as it was swept up into the channel between the huge cement piers that cleaved the strong tides and provided stripers with an ambush point on the quieter down tide side of said obstacle.

At certain stages near the slack tides the bass would come to the surface and feed on bait-fish drawn to the overhead lights on the center span. On these occasions our plugs, jigs and the modest assortment of live and artificial baits in our possession were usually unable to "match the hatch." After one such night of unconditional frustration I decided to pack it in early to get a head start on the normally productive early morning tide at the rocky cove immediately south of the bridge which almost always rewarded us with a few market fish in the 8 to 16 pound class. Disgustedly I flipped my last cigarette into the channel then watched it drift from the light into the shadow. A huge boil erupted under the butt sucking it under the surface with a loud whoosh. "Did you see that?" I asked my partner. "No but I heard it." We sat there for the remainder of the tide and studied the activity. After numerous attempts I managed to hook a five pound fish on a small Bill Upperman white bucktail which I jig-walked down the pier just under the surface. The fish was lip hooked at best and his trashing against the tight drag caused the hook to tear free. We'd seen enough and were convinced we were much closer to a solution. We visited our mutual friend Del Thurston, the tender on the Brightman Street Bridge, and a fisherman who wore many hats, hoping to solicit his fly rod.

The affable and generous Del not only complied but agreed to tie several large white streamers for us. We visited the bridge the following night and continued our education. We started out with four streamers and a willowy fresh water trout rod. At the conclusion of this brief operation it was stripers five, fishermen nothing. We lost the four flies to the bass and in frustrated desperation I choked up too tight on the line and broke the rod at the ferrule. Our efforts with the standard conventional tackle produced two bass in the 10 pound class but nothing like the action with the streamers. It was back to the drawing board. My friend Roland was on the phone the following day tracking down the heaviest of salmon rods he could locate. We went through an assortment of tackle, including one beautiful Orvis rod, which was never intended for the catwalks of that rusty draw bridge that cracked like the report of a rifle when Roland refused to allow a muscular bass to dump the last few feet of backing from the tiny reel. We finally settled on a couple of heavy Shakespeare Wonder rods (model FY-930) for weight forward 9 line, fitted with Pflueger medalist reels loaded up with all the heavy mono backing we could stuff onto those knuckle busters.

Even these stout outfits were no match for the occasional behemoth, which comparable to the proverbial troll that lived under the story tale bridge, surged upward and away towing our offerings out into the abyss of Mt. Hope Bay. Tackle and methods have come a long way since that time and the historic Slades Ferry Bridge has long since given way to the progress of dynamite and the wrecking ball. I still own that old Shakespeare along with a couple of Berkley fly rods and an assortment of other fly fishing tackle yet I still don't consider myself a fly fishermen. Over the last 30 years I've guided a number of fly fishermen as well as those who aspire to be fly fishermen "to" some of the largest fish they had ever tangled with. "TO" is the operative word. I've left a trail of busted tackle, broken hearts, and a few trophies which grace the walls of the accomplished anglers who kept their cool while hanging on for dear life. Those accounts would fill up the pages of a small book and are best saved for some quiet winter afternoon whiling away time in a boat show booth. Much has changed since those primitive beginnings, but in the absence of major geographic and ecological alteration, fish still return to those productive locations which I'm sure have held fish since man first pursued them by damming rivers, setting nets, casting handlines, right up to the present day mechanics of the rod and reel. The very same places I found fish holding in 50 years ago still provide resting and feeding stops for the descendants of today's migrants.

Fly fishing is not about looking down at other angling practices, owning the most expensive tackle or dressing like some exorbitantly priced mannequin out of an L.L. Bean or Orvis catalog. It is about getting back in touch with nature, stalking the salt water flats and experiencing the thrill of a fish rising to your hand crafted feathered offering. If I could fool big stripers with a pipe cleaner and some bucktail wrapped around a 3/0 hook imagine what you could do with an artistically crafted silverside pattern worked along the edge of the eel grass on the bottom of the outgoing tide. I should warn you that this pastime has been known to cause absence and tardiness from work and other scheduled engagements, nervous exhaustion, preoccupation with tide charts and solunar tables along with complaints from neglected spouses, companions and employers. For this reason all fly fishing gear should be appropriately labeled - CAUTION! This exercise can be habit forming.

CHARLEY BATTLES A STRIPER AT DUSK ON HIS HOME WATERS ON COLES RIVER. STRIPER FISHING WITH A FLY ROD AT DUSK IS A DEADLY METHOD OF FOOLING LEGAL SIZED STRIPERS.

LIGHTS OUT

INTO THE DARKNESS

Whoever suggested that nothing good ever happens after 2:00 AM was most definitely never engaged in the nocturnal pursuit of striped bass. Although the bulk of my fishing these days takes place sometime well before sunrise until just after sunset that has not always been the case although that was seldom by choice. During the early stages of my fishing career I worked from 8 to 5 PM and by the time I returned home, gulped down supper and headed off to the ocean, it was usually less than an hour to go before sunset. That of course, was not a bad thing. My fishing partner Russ lived for what he referred to as the witching hour right after the sun slipped behind the horizon when that period of deep purple transition provided some of the most exciting fishing of our lifetime. I'm always keenly aware of the hurried flights of gulls and cormorants that begin making their way back to their secure island roosts because that usually coincides with the larger fish initiating their inshore movement. Although I am a huge proponent of daytime striper fishing I am also well aware of the difficulty of locating and tempting larger specimens during the months of July and August when daytime temperatures reach and exceed 90-degrees.

Many years ago on a steamy late July day I made plans with a friend to fish a late afternoon tide along a stretch of ocean between Westport Harbor MA and Sakonnet Point RI. I recall the gauge outside the boat shed reading 94 in the shade at 3:30 in the afternoon. My bride came out of the house as I was hooking up the trailer to my tow vehicle and informed me that my deckmate had a family emergency and could not make the trip. My apprehensive wife suggested that I ditch the trip and get an early start in the morning. I was sweating from the effort of hooking up the boat and with a cooler full of ice and fourteen big bass eels on ice I was not about to abort the trip. I assured her that with calm seas and very little wind I would be home early so I packed my duffel and headed for Sakonnet. The only traffic on the road was a steady stream of cars reluctantly leaving the cooler environment of the ocean and heading back to the oppressive heat of the city and suburbs. Surprisingly for that time of year there were only two other trailers in the parking lot when I launched and headed around the islands on my way to an area of submerged boulders a mile and a half away. Surface water temperature was holding at 74, a bit warm for that area but I knew it was much more comfortable 34 feet below. I worked that area over thoroughly with a very tempting live eel to no avail then at sunset I moved off to work a few more spikes to the east. At the second location I fed that perfect snake to a hungry yellow eyed chopper so I beat a hasty retreat rather than waste my precious bait on bluefish. This was well before the advent of GPS and cell phones when the embodiment of being out alone in the dark meant just that - alone. Time passes quickly after dark and that night was no exception. I moved from location to location with my supply of eels dwindling precipitously from assaults of smaller stripers and the occasional chopper. I only hooked one quality fish that night but it was the kind of encounter you never forget. Everyone has at least one big fish story but I guess I might be a bit in front of that threshold because I have quite a few.

I made that connection a few hours after sunset at the first location I had worked and it began rather inauspiciously. At the end of a drift I began a slow retrieve and felt a slight bump, the type of hit similar to all of the previous bass earlier that evening. After twenty minutes of casting and drifting that eel was pretty well spent so I dipped the rod and engaged the clutch as the fish slowly moved off with the bait and as soon as that hook took hold all hell broke loose. Of all the stripers I've been connected to this was the very first jumbo that came right to the surface, broke water and shook her head and rattled her gills like a tarpon. If I were a superstitious person I might have thought she was trying to scare me. What followed was a protracted brawl fought in her domain and on her terms. She was not your typical striper - the type that is content to make a few powerful runs before fatigue sets in and makes her more controllable. This fish ran off all my main line and induced a sick feeling when I felt the backing knot bump ominously through the guides. I was using the best tackle I could afford which consisted of a stout seven foot boat rod with a Penn Jigmaster spooled with new 30-pound Handy line connected to last years' 30-pound line used as backing. Money was always a consideration. I battled that fish for what seemed like an eternity which in all probability was no more than five or six minutes. I chased her whenever I could and held on and prayed when she headed for the minefield of boulders that was her primary escape route. What transpired was the perfect parallel to gaining an inch and losing a yard. I harbor this conviction that trophy fish that survive to live that long are cunning specimens that have survived numerous encounters with man and nature which has honed their instincts.

Despite the pressure she made numerous runs and on occasions turned the little bass boat completely around with the awesome power of her broad tail. After two strong thrusts for the bottom when she first saw my hull she finally rolled on the surface close enough for me to lunge with the gaff. Once more she displayed her awesome power while I held on for dear life. In my unsteady condition I could not lift her into the boat so we drifted for a while with the gaff in her side and my left forearm jammed into her cavernous maw. On my next attempt I heaved for all I was worth and rolled her over the rail and onto the deck. There was just enough light for me to examine her length and wide girth and up to that time she was the largest striper I had ever caught. The next day my trophy striper was officially weighed in at my bass club at 58-pounds, 8 ounces which was only good enough for second place because my friend's 64 was at the top of the leader board and held on to take top honors that year. Over the seasons I've heard of some supposed experts who presume that night fishing is unfair to the quarry. Not so. The only human advantage of night fishing is the potential for increased hookups but those fish do not lose their way or become confused in the dark. They are in fact nocturnal hunters that thrive under the cover of darkness. And anyone who suggests it is less sporting to hunt for stripers when the lights go out doesn't know what the hell they are talking about! Even on what we refer to as the black moons there is usually sufficient light to pick out landmarks and ranges but even after decades of night fishing in my most familiar surroundings there is always the chance I might be spending the night on the water when thick fog rolls in and makes it too dangerous to move between the boulders and reefs to make my way home.

On more black nights than I would like to admit my greed overcame my good judgment and I overstayed my welcome. The once very familiar shoreline begins to look and sound alike in dense fog and I have spent many a damp and dismal night on the anchor waiting for daylight and at least fifty yards of precious visibility to inch my way back to the harbor. One night Russ Malone and I had fish stacked up motor box high in the cockpit of my little Hinckley bass boat when the fog began to roll in. "Two more fish" my deckmate promised. He was correct but those two jumbos cost us a good night sleep. At the time we were bullet proof and overconfident because of over forty years combined experience between us in that gnarly environment but in my dread to avoid the breakers and bearded boulders on the outside corner of safe passage I cheated that compass course that usually took us directly to the opening and ended up in the maze of boulders that all looked alike in the thick black fog. After a half hour of going in circles we grudgingly set the anchor and snuggled up with our catch. A few hours later the sound of the anchor line straining in the chock caused me to jump up startled to find a gusty northwest wind had devoured the fog. We discovered we were a scant fifteen yards from the deeper passage that would have taken us to open water and a straight northeast course into the harbor. Fishing when the lights go out is not for everyone but for those intrepid anglers who invest the time and effort to become comfortable in the deep purple there is seldom any going back.

I have had numerous clients who aspired to learn how to successfully fish night tide but once out there on that dark and unfamiliar ocean, had second thoughts. There is no doubt that all the familiar landmarks and ranges that brought them confidence during the period between sunrise and sunset had gradually ghosted away leaving them in a confusing and sometimes mysterious arena making them very uncomfortable. Fishing in the dark, even in familiar locations, causes many to be overcome by that prickly feeling of anxiety yet after a few favorable experiences most fishermen overcome them.

Linesiders in First Place

Linesiders Bass Club of this city has taken over first place in the R. J. Scheafer salt water fishing contest.

Herb Dickinson, John Vivelros, Roland Coulombe, Larry Szczesney, Charles Soares, Ernie Rogers, Joe Soares and Russ Malone of the FR. club made the stripers and blues count for their advance to the top spot in the 18th annual competition.

Dickinson's 64 pound, 4 ounce striper is the heaviest of 22 50-pounders taken so far this season. It was hauled in at Cuttyhunk from the Jigster.

Charley Soares got one weighing 58 pounds, 8 ounces from his boat, Piscator, and Viveiros boated a 52-pounder from Capt. Frank Sabatowski's June Bug.

Intrepid Striper Club of Wrentham moved into second place with 56, 54 and 50 pound stripers, and Cape Cod Salties retained third place by bagging stripers from Pleasant Bay and Chatham.

Massachusetts Striped Bass Association of Wollaston is fourth, and Long Beach Island Fishing Club of Cedars, N.J., fifth.

Central Connecticut Club of Meriden is sixth, Mayflower Anglers of Squantum, seventh; B and D Fishing Club, Brooklyn, N.Y., eighth; New Haven Sportsmen's Club, ninth, and Norwich (Conn.) Striper Club, 10th.

Runnerup to Dickinson's fish is a 62-pounder bagged last weekend by Lou Stupelli of the Babylon Tuna Club.

Everyone has a big fish story whether it's about a win or a loss. The author has gaffed numerous 50 and a couple of 60's but he never hooked a fish like this 58 pound striper that battled like a crazed tarpon. Fishing after dark has its downsides but for those who master it the potential for jumbo bass is unlimited.

CHAPTER V

PROVEN METHODS FOR SUCCESFUL ANGLING

JEFF BRANCO WITH A HUSKY STRIPER HE LANDED FISHING WITH THE AUTHOR ON A SULTRY MID AUGUST DAY IN 2014. THIS WAS ONE OF OVER 20 FISH IN EXCESSS OF 35 POUNDS THEY CAUGHT DURING THE DAYLIGHT HOURS USING CHARLEY'S TUBE AND WORM METHOD.

TROLLING TACTICS

THE ESSENTIAL METHOD FOR LOCATING AND CATCHING FISH

Trolling is one of the most productive methods of catching fish and not the boring practice some would have you think it to be. You can set up on an anchor and ladle chum over the side and wait for the fish to come to you or you can troll proven lures over productive habitat to locate fish. Some of the critics of trolling are tuna fishermen who sit at anchor all day creating a chum slick to lure tuna to their boat and often return to port without so much as a sighting for their efforts. Trolling not only allows you to move and hunt fish but it provides you a better working knowledge of fish habitat and permits you to familiarize yourself with structure and shorelines. After years of working boat and marine trade shows I continually run into fishermen who won't or don't troll because they claim its monotonous and as soon as I hear those words I know I'm talking with someone who does not know how, what or where to troll. Leaving Westport Harbor and putting out the lines once you pass the channel markers is not trolling. You have to put your lures and baits over productive bottom, the type of structure that attracts and holds fish because it provides cover for them. Too many fishermen who troll over barren or plain vanilla bottom never catch fish and give this method a bad name. There are numerous ingredients that combine to make trolling successful and the following discussion touches on just a few of them.

The size and design of your boat can make a huge difference between success and failure. Bigger is not always better particularly when you are hunting stripers in their rocky lairs. Smaller, shallow draft, open bass boats are preferred to larger sport fishermen or cruising type boats because of their maneuverability and unimpeded 360-degree visibility. The sound of your engines and the shadow your boat casts in this habitat also has a great deal to do with your prosperity. Stealth is as important when hunting large stripers in the boulder fields they frequent as it is to hunters stalking big and small game in the woods and fields. You can't expect to make a lot of noise and cast large shadows over structure and expect the fish to sit tight and wait for whatever you might happen to be trolling behind you to come along. Divers who have spent hundreds of hours observing fish in their natural habitat have reported that fish, primarily predators, are very sensitive of foreign noises and shadows. That is just one reason why I never troll up tight to structure but rather move in such a fashion so as not to cast the shadow of my hull over the areas where the fish are holding.

One of the most frequent questions I'm asked about trolling the tube and worm combo is "how many Rpm's do you run to attain what you consider optimum or the desired speed?" There is no correct answer to that question because there is no way to make a comparison between our engines, hull shape, currents, wind and all the other variables that affect our trolling speed. Speed or lack of it is critical for success when trolling any type of lure or baits. After almost five decades of experimenting I've determined that fish will strike tubes fished along the bottom of the water column if they are moved along at fewer than three knots with two knots close to the ideal speed. I don't believe you can troll a tube too slow but you certainly can move one too fast. My experiments were always conducted under controlled conditions, or at least as controlled as you could have them under the changing conditions of this liquid environment. Experimenting when the fish are not biting or present won't provide you with much more than frustration. When we were into fish and they were readily striking tubes trolled at two knots we increased the speed to three knots and while we were still catching fish the action fell off considerably from our two-knot runs.

Advancing our speed to four knots turned off the larger fish but a few schoolies continued to chase and hit our tubes. Can you catch fish trolling tubes over three knots? Of course you can but trolling your lures low and slow will usually produce the most action. When I first began fishing these lures I began to measure my speed by the feel of the tube going through the water and later by the speed indicated by the calculations on my GPS. Over the years I've fished with anglers who prefer different methodologies and have found that by fishing my tubes slowly and in the strike zone (the area from the bottom to about four feet up) we continually outfished the twisty tubes that swim faster and higher in the water column. Although there are numerous baits you can stick at the end of your tube the most productive and popular is the sandworm. To prove my point I'd ask you to take a large sea worm (clamworm) then place it in the bottom of a bucket of salt water to observe its action. The worm does not gyrate or spin and twist as some lures are geared to do, it moves through the water like an eel or a snake crawling along the ground. If you can duplicate the action of the worm on the business end of your tube you will begin to realize the rewards.

It's a proven fact that the slower you troll the more naturally you present your baits and the more hits they will produce. Let's assume you have a Penn 330 GTI loaded with backing and five colors of 36-pound test lead line and a six or seven foot hollow glass boat rod with a fast taper action. Tie your 15 feet of clear leader material from the lead line directly onto your tube and attach the largest sea worm you can purchase to the business end of the hook. Adjust the depth of your lure by allowing it to bump the bottom then reel in a few feet to insure your lure is working at the depth where the fish are feeding. I prefer to hold the rod in my hand to determine if the lure is running clean or if panfish in the form of scup, sea bass or tautog are chasing and attacking the worm. Fishermen who put their rods in the holders and then turn their back on them to look forward will never know if they have picked up weed or been stripped (skinned) by smaller fish. By holding the rod you will develop a sensitivity that will provide you with information as to how your tube is swimming and whether or not small fish have nibbled your worm off the hook. There is nothing more frustrating than to make the perfect pass over structure holding large stripers and have a scup remove the worm from the hook before the lure reaches its destination. Although it's easier and much more comfortable to stick your rods in the holders and concentrate on your progress along the water than to hold the rod in your hand, the difference in productivity is well worth a bit of discomfort. Trolling is one of my favorite methods of locating and catching large predators and I'll bet if you give this method a fair chance it will become yours as well.

GOING DEEP

FISHING BELOW THE EDGE

The bottom line on the paper chart recorder traced the tip of the ridge then began gradually spiraling downward as the gentle northwest breeze pushed us offshore and down the rocky slope. We were targeting tautog in late October a time when most of the larger stripers were migrating westward along our rugged New England coastline. Two hours previous to our bottom probing we'd plugged up a dozen westward bound schoolies satisfying our compulsion to extend the bass season up through the first few frosty days of November. A few choggies had begun nibbling on the exposed sections of the green crabs when I felt at solid strike that snapped the rod down and almost jarred it from my grip. Unlike the double tap of a white chinner this fish hit and ran so I reared back and set the 4/0 Kirby. At the sting of the hook the fish ran off 50-feet of line on the moderate drag setting until I made a slight adjustment and was able to stop the run before the fish took off on yet another sideways sweep. Looking up at the recorder I noticed three targets at 58-feet, some four feet above the 63-foot gray-line bottom level. This fish was no tautog. Andy set his rod in the holder and walked over to admire the arch in the rod as line peeled off the now stiffened drag. Because of the size of the hooks I gave the fish a bit more leeway than I would have liked but it was tiring and the runs were now reduced to stubborn circles off the port stern.

The first sign of color revealed a long silver fish with dark black stripes which my mate slipped the big net under. Flopping on the deck with the black tog hook firmly set in its jaw was a 32-pound linesider that had taken a shine to a green crab on the half shell. Andy turned then bolted for the stern where his rod was bent and the spool on his jigmaster was giving up line like he was hooked onto a westbound freighter. The white paper on the chart recorder methodically marked its way down a slope that fell off from 33 to 79-feet showing targets along the drop holding a just a few feet off the bottom. Andy bested his fish in less time and in short order we were admiring a brace of husky linesiders that had been grubbing along the side of a gradual slope located a considerable distance offshore from the famed striper fishing grounds off Newport's Ocean Drive. Prior to that incident I'd routinely captured stripers in depths from 32 to 54-feet and occasionally a bit deeper in the holes off Devil's Bridge which along with the Race in New York were both locations where stripers and blues were extricated from nosebleed depths approaching 180-feet. We didn't catch another striper that day but when I filleted the bass at home I found several juvenile tautogs, some jumbo cunners and a few Jonah crabs in their stomachs.

Although we intercepted a few more legal stripers along Newport's Ocean Drive that season I spent considerable time and effort working up a deep water strategy for the next season and made plans to employ them once the inshore water temperatures warmed up in July and August. Fishermen are creatures of habit and because many of us began fishing from the beaches and caught fish within the range of our casts we adapted to this near-shore mentality about where to locate stripers. That is the root cause of surf fishermen casting out as far as their equipment and talent will allow while anglers from boats cast toward the rockpiles along the shores. When this mindset prevails we subconsciously rule out hunting stripers in their deep water lairs and persist in working the near shore waters even throughout the warm summer months when the larger specimens are usually just a short distance away. Since that day of the green crab stripers I religiously dedicate time to examine and explore a few of my favorite striper deep water cavities on each trip after a morning of pre-dawn plugging or casting eels into the white water washes. In order to appreciate searching cooler and more protected waters for stripers it's necessary to understand that deep is a relative term.

One foggy morning I was trolling along the top of the hump off Squibnocket where we typically begin jigging with deadly two ounce Rich Andrus parachutes. This is usually a busy location however once the current begins to haul the other boats begin dropping out and moving off but it's seldom because the fish have stopped eating. At the beginning of the change of tide those two-ounce chutes are tending bottom and being presented to fish in the strike zone however once the current begins to pull the fish seek deeper structure out from under the influence of the most powerful currents which is when it becomes necessary to snap on a three or four ounce jig and move off to the down-tide ambush locations that big stripers prefer when it becomes too strenuous to work up against the currents. After fishing a location for an extended period of time it becomes apparent to the savvy angler

118

as to where to look for fish at various stages of the tide particularly those periods when the currents are pulling hardest and causing the fish to move off to set up new ambush points. As most other boats headed off to other locations we moved off the shoals in the 17 to 13 foot depths to the edges where the bottom drops off from 24 to 33-feet. Switching the two ounce off for four ounce chutes we began fishing along the edge and continued to catch at a rate as good as or better than earlier in the tide. We only increased our depth about 20-feet however that drop made the difference between steaming to a new location in search of fish and staying right in the area and hooking up until the tide went slack.

Another example of the importance of becoming familiar with probing the depths is the various choices that are available when fishing locations in Vineyard Sound, Buzzards Bay and Long Island Sound. Late last July there were bass and bluefish breaking all around Norton Point and the nearby section of the Vineyard north shore. Those fish were feeding on fine bait in the form of juvenile silversides and other small baitfish the size of which do not usually interest larger stripers. We moved off just outside the contour line between 28 and 44-feet which with the prevailing south wind took us into depths of 60 to 80-feet. We were fishing live eels on three-way rigs and catching bass from 22 to 34-pounds that were feeding on much larger forage. When we pulled into Menemsha later that afternoon we opened the bass up and found juvenile scup to 9-inches, numerous sea robins, an 11-inch fluke, lobsters and sand crabs and the remains of other fish that appeared to be juvenile tautogs and scup. The heavier bass were not only holding in the cooler more comfortable water they were expending much less energy and feeding on larger forage. I've fished this same area during one of the John Havlicek tournaments when live herring was an option and we caught bass from the mid 20 to 30-pound class fishing herring off Norton Rock in 75-feet of water. I certainly believe those same bass make forays into the shoreline at night where they are able to push and trap larger prey up against the beaches but under a hot mid-day sun the larger specimens can be found in depths up to 90-feet and deeper.

The name of the game is keeping your eyes on the screen. Regardless of what you name them be it sonar, fish finders, or chart recorders keep your eyes on the screen for icons or targets because they will put you on fish attracting structure which will often result in finding larger stripers. Turn down the sensitivity for more accurate readings and don't pay attention to all those fish icons on your screen, particularly if the gain is turned up high because they will frustrate the hell out of you. Finding the fish is only half of the equation; once you locate them you have to make them eat. So many fishermen I speak with report finding larger fish in deep water but bemoan not being able to catch them and I believe I know why. Although bass will not always strike at a lure or bait that doesn't mean they won't eat. In order to give yourself and the location you are fishing your best possible effort you have to be fishing in the strike zone. Anglers that are successfully fishing the 80-foot plus depths off Gay Head or the deep water between the north shore of the Vineyard in the trough between Lucas Shoal and Middle Ground know they have to keep their offerings working along the bottom. Using a three-way rig or a heavy bucktail while stemming the tide is one way to determine if you are hitting bottom and are fishing in the strike zone. Far too many fishermen locate the fish but are not presenting their offering naturally along the bottom. I'm well aware that predators will come way up off the bottom to chase large plugs, jigs, or umbrella rigs however its those same lures fished just a few feet off the bottom that will consistently catch more and larger stripers. Going deep is not for everyone. If you are satisfied with your results and production fishing along the inside contour lines I have no intention of tempting you out of your comfort zone. If you're serious about hanging bigger fish, particularly during sticky weather, try working the deep holes during the middle of the day along the structure changes illustrated on any chart of the areas you fish and this will result in opportunities at linesiders you'd otherwise never have an occasion to present a lure to.

THIS IS AN IMAGE THAT CAN TAKE YOUR BREATH AWAY. A HUGE SCHOOL OF STRIPERS IS TEARING INTO BAIT JUST BEHIND THE COVER OF A NATURAL OBSTRUCTION. THIS IS NOT THE RESULT OF TOO MUCH GAIN AND FALSE ICONS BECAUSE THE AUTHOR USUALLY HAS HIS MACHINES SET AT MINIMUM GAIN IN SHALLOW WATER.

CASTING AND TROLLING PLUGS

THE ALLURE OF ARTIFICIALS

With the risk of sounding over confident I can almost guarantee catching a limit of legal bass with my preferred bait in the form of live eels or my tube and worm rigs on just about every trip out during the course of a season. While the vast majority of the largest bass I have ever captured fell for some form of bait, the most memorable catches were those big cows that were fooled with artificial lures. When I first began fishing my objective was to catch every legal bass I could locate to take to market, and then some years later it was all about the size of the bass I could fool. For the record, I am not at all averse to tempting and capturing big fish with live bait but if I have my way and a deckmate or client with a similar proclivity for floating lumber, we begin the pre-dawn hours tossing big wood for stripers. Some of you who have read my books might recall one of my early childhood mentors whose slogan was "if you want to catch big fish you gotta feed-um meat." I took that edict to heart and have enjoyed a very productive career fishing with live bait. For decades I was living large in what master plug maker Danny Pichney referred to as a successful "live bait rut." The man who I referred to as the Ghepetto of salt water plug building persuaded me to turn that essential corner and I have never looked back.

When Tim Coleman first brought Danny to my house, I was netting pogies in Padanaram Harbor and catching stripers around Cuttyhunk and the Vineyard via live lining and trolling baits on wire line. Danny showed up with two New York market grocery bags full of his signature plugs. He paid for his first meal of chouricio and chips and an overnight stay in the day bed in my office with a generous gift of the lures that Coleman had been bragging about for years. Our first trip embarked from Padanaram Harbor where we located a large school of menhaden where Coleman and I made short work of filling the baitwell with lively pogies. Twenty minutes later after Pichney politely declined a rod, the editor and I were hooked up to teen sized stripers. On our second pass the plug maker requested permission to float a plug off the stern. I couldn't understand why a man of his reputation with decades of fishing experience would want to troll a plug between two of the most deadly striper live baits known to man but I nodded in the affirmative and continued the pass after elbowing Coleman in the ribs. Less than two minutes later Coleman returned the favor with a painful jab and a nod toward the stern. There was our guest on his knees with his trusty Harnel rod bent in a near perfect arc. We hurriedly recovered our baits and made way for our guest to battle his fish. That feisty 20-pound striper came alongside with a mottled blue Danny sub-surface swimmer stuck in the corner of its jaw. That was the beginning of a long and lasting love affair with that special man and his life-like creations.

Many an enjoyable and productive trip followed for that same trio of anglers only on most occasions we pushed off a bit earlier minus the live bait. On the last trip with Danny I recall we fished the north side of the Vineyard and Devil's Bridge with only two bass in the 18-pound class to show for our efforts. We had been up since 3:00AM so at mid afternoon I pulled into Menemsha and navigated the skinny water up into the salt pond. Coleman began cranking Z's as soon as the anchor bit so the old timer and I sat around the console and chatted about our mutual infatuation. I promised him that the fishing would be much better on the change of the tide to which the man from frenzied New York replied; "Now that I'm finally here it feels like I've died and gone to heaven." The evening bite wasn't just better it was fantastic. We took bass up to 36 pounds at a time when specimens that size were considered the peak of the biomass. The first bass were fooled by his surface swimmers cast into the huge boulders under the rim of the multihued cliffs at Gay Head and the remainder out on the rip where the fish committed suicide over his throbbing sub surface swimmers. Tired and hungry we made the long but enjoyable ride back to Padanaram where we searched long and hard for an all night diner. Danny and Tim headed back to Mystic and New York but the old timer left me much more than a shopping bag full of plugs; he reignited an appreciation and passion for the appeal and application of skillfully presented artificial lures.

Since that providential meeting I have enjoyed the challenge and satisfaction of fooling stripers with finely crafted artificial lures. My supply of original Danny plugs has dwindled but I still have a few that show the scars of stripers and blues and a few that have never tasted salt water. Today I am always on the lookout for both new and old lures that were designed to fool big stripers. Many of the veteran plugs I have rescued were found in garages and basements once occupied by retired or deceased fishermen. Some of my most rewarding finds were discovered strung between the rafters on electrical and copper wire that stretched from one wall to the other in the dank windowless basement of some old three tenement houses. One old waterman invited me over to his cellar and began extolling the virtues of his homemade still and the gin clear liquid that dripped from the copper tubing at the bitter end. In one corner there was a coal bin and in the other a root cellar that held a pile of potatoes and several varieties of squash. The wooden wall that separated the cellar units was covered in cobwebs but underneath I spied a large treble hook. Further investigation led to the discovery of five giant Creek Chub Pikes in various stages of deterioration. All but one plug had rusted hooks with bruises and bites from bluefish and battles in the boulders with runaway linesiders. Permission was granted to liberate them from their indefinite detention and after a few minutes of bartering I was on my way with a great find.

The newer of those plugs was a big pearl pike that had seen little if any use and soon became a favorite. The first time I cast that plug was on a windy night up inside the rocks off Westport Harbor's Elephant Rock Beach in what was a providential moment. My medium weight spinning outfit was taxed to the max with the weight of that plug but halfway to the boat it was assaulted by a wild eyed teen sized striper. Russ Malone, my fishing partner at that time, told me that plug was a hunk of wooden destiny and it turns out that he was correct. For two seasons I lobbed that seductive chunk of wood into striper lairs and it rewarded me with numerous muscle fish, a few of which won me treasure in the R.J. Schaeffer Saltwater fishing contest. Years later with Editor Tim Coleman on deck I cast that plug into a boulder field and hooked onto one of those stripers that were never meant to be landed; fighting it for several minutes until it scuffed and broke my heavy leader. In retrospect that visit to the old timer's basement was an auspicious episode in the pursuit of my undying passion. Today some of my most enjoyable and productive fishing outings are when I am casting the remainder of my prized original Danny's and the seductive creations of Gibbs, Asylum and Huey lures. In this era where live bait fishing is one of the most predominant techniques being employed, if you aren't considering or including the application of artificial lures you are missing out on a rewarding and productive technique. If you are lucky enough to be invited into an old fisherman's basement and discover some secreted fishing treasure but are too shy to make an offer or attempt at bartering, please call me, I have no such compulsions.

ASK JOHN MUELLER AND RON RUDOWSKY ABOUT THE SATISFACTION OF CASTING ARTIFICIAL LURES. BOTH OF THESE TROPHY STRIPERS WERE HARD WON ON A DAY WHEN THE FISH HAD LOCKJAW UNTIL A WEATHER SHIFT TURNED THEM ON. FOOLING FISH WITH PLUGS IS REWARDING.

DRESSING PLUGS WITH HACKLES

A TAIL OF TWO PLUGS

His plug hit the wash before I'd even had the opportunity to reach for my rod. Although I always offer my deckmates the first toss his premature cast caught me a bit off guard. His big white surface swimmer began its retreat from the foaming white water swishing, gurgling and wagging its tail. My plug, the exact same model and color, was in the air when I spotted a boil behind his plug so I turned back to tell him. It was at that moment that I noticed that he was committing a mortal sin of plug casting. He wasn't looking at his lure but toward the adjacent reef where he was already planning his second cast. My cast launched my plug deeper into the back eddy on the opposite side of the wash and turned the handle on the conventional to initiate my retrieve. The plug was invisible in the roiling foam however a striper, with a keen sense of hearing along with a sensitive lateral line, struck the head of the lure and with a sweep of its broad tail at the bite of the hook she began taking line. I set the hook, once then again for good measure before I turned the fish which headed out of the cauldron behind the reef out into deeper water. Lowering the rod, lifting up then reeling back down I determined that this was not a big striper but a muscular bass full of fight and savoring the chilly oxygen rich spring ocean water. Before my fish surfaced I looked aft to observe my mate make his third cast to the same location my fish came from and once again there was the tell-tale boil of a stripers dorsal in the wake of his plug. I notified him of the interest but he didn't see the fish because he was much too interested in watching me. Casting plugs is not nuclear physics but it does require experience and close awareness to your lures.

For the record this man was, at least by his own admission, an experienced surf caster with numerous braggin' sized stripers to his credit. From my limited observations his so-called proficiency appeared to be little more than overstated self promotion. I learned to cast artificial lures, from the ubiquitous bucktail to rough turned wooden plugs, the difficult way through trial and error without any assistance from the few experienced anglers of the day, men who wouldn't give a wide-eyed kid the time of day. If half of the fish that followed, bumped or slapped my offerings had been hooked I'd most likely be totally worn out and used up at this juncture of my life but as one of my grey beard mentors was fond of saying, "too soon; old-too late smart". By the time I hooked and released my third fish, a handsome 12-pound specimen, my deckmate was beginning to come unglued. At least he wasn't completely bereft of common sense, he was aware that there was inequality in our success but he wasn't attentive enough to figure out what it was. I make every effort to help other fisherman recalling the difficulties of my early years but there is a fine line that is often difficult to cross. Some fishermen, no matter how much assistance they may require, become offended if you offer suggestions so now I usually wait until they ask for help. With three fish to his none the man wasn't at all bashful. "What the hell are you doing" he asked, "we're using the exact same plugs and working them slowly but I can't buy a strike." I reached over and grabbed his plug and held it up alongside my own. He looked at them quizzically and still didn't notice what to me was a glaring difference was. While he was looking for something major he didn't notice that his lure was fitted with the builders standard treble while I had altered my plug by removing the treble and replacing it with a 5/0 live bait hook tied with a thick wrapping of long lively white hackle. When I pointed this out to him he was puzzled because he didn't believe that slight variation could have made that much difference.

At this point I was damn near disinclined to discuss this any further but I thought of his long suffering mother who had been so good to me and I showed him the bottle of scent I carried in my shirt pocket. "I thought you were wiping your plug with that cloth- is that stuff any good? I suggested the combination of hackles and scent was good enough to account for three fish to his none to which he reluctantly nodded in agreement. To take it one step further I asked him to place his lure in the water alongside my own as I slipped the gear shift into forward and began slow trolling. The brace of plugs moved enticingly only my lure was longer and the bucktail provided a much more seductive wriggle. Although I had not anointed the tail with scent in the last six casts there was still a trace of sheen emanating from the wrap. My theory, translated into a stripers thought process, was that our lures looked alike but his didn't incite the striper to attack. On the other hand my lure looked like a baitfish, wriggled like an injured fish and gave off the authentic scent of food. That sealed the deal. In most locations we only get one or perhaps two casts into a productive area so why not make certain that your presentation is up to the task of fooling a potential trophy striper. Swim your plug alongside before you cast it into productive locations. This will allow you to determine the speed of your retrieve and just how fast you can pop and gurgle a plug that is being sized up by a striper without the lure rolling over or jerking instead of it moving through the water naturally.

The longer hackle not only presents a larger more seductive offering it also affords the ease and safety of removing hooks and releasing fish without a swinging treble to dig into your person. If you can't find large tied hackles buy some hackle material and tie your own. There is no such thing as an award for tying the perfect saltwater plug hackle. Remember our quarry is wild, typically opportunistic predators, not educated trout in a heavily fished book or stream. If it looks good to you it probably looks good to stripers and if you're up to it I respectfully suggest cheating with a carefully applied natural scent that will enhance your presentation.

THE ADDITION OF BUCKTAILS OR CHARLEY'S PREFERENCE OF LONGER HACKLES DEFINITELY ENHANCES THE ATTRACTION OF A PLUG. THE STANDARD WAY PLUGS ARE SOLD IS WITH A TREBLE AT THE REAR BUT THE AUTHOR REMOVES THE TREBLE AND REPLACES IT WITH A SINGLE HOOK. HE ALSO ADDS SCENT AND PREFERS THE BIO-EDGE SCENTS IN BUNKER, HERRING AND SQUID.

THE MAGIC OF EELS

FISHING WITH SERPENTS THROUGH THE DECADES

God hath no fury like this burglarized eel man. Albert's philosophy was to live and let live but God help anyone that he caught stealing from him. There were tales and rumors about the retribution he extracted from thieves and bullies and according to the caretaker and the elders they were far from exaggerations. The eel man was a retired merchant seaman who lived on a small pension and the income he derived from his string of eel pots. During the winter months he hooked up with another veteran and worked in that man's construction business. Long before the body building craze Albert had a physique like the Charles Atlas character used in magazine ads although his was the result of hard work and good living. He ate just about everything that came from the sea, and while he enjoyed a nip now and then, he always took his liquor in moderation. I can still see him in his blue denim shirts, cuffs rolled up to huge biceps and the top three buttons open exposing a hairy chest and rock solid pectorals. I had always admired him from afar and although he was cordial toward me I had very little interaction with him until that early Saturday morning.

While turning over rocks and scratching for clams I heard the sharp whistle and turned to see Albert on the boathouse porch waving to me. The first thing I noticed was that his left arm was in a sling but his right arm beckoned and I believed he was hailing me to run an errand for him. "Hey kid, do you want to go for a boat ride?" Looking over his shoulder I saw the caretaker nodding in the affirmative so I agreed to go for what would be the first of many such boat rides. He had injured his left wing helping his construction buddy tearing down a cement block wall and he would be unable to row out to his boat or use both hands to pull his pots. Rowing came naturally to me but that morning my nerves got the best of me causing me to try too hard. This was my audition and I was well aware of it so after a few blown strokes I spun the punt around smartly and put it right where he could board from the stern. He hauled his gear aboard while I swapped the mooring lines from the workboat to the tender, waiting for him to choke and fire up the temperamental Scott Atwater outboard bolted on the stern. There was a combination of rainwater and salt seep in the bilge which I quickly dispensed with using the wooden scoops he fashioned with scrap lumber from the nearby Clarkson's boat house. Waste not; want not was much more than just a slogan back then.

I'd like to report that I could recall every moment of that first trip hauling Albert's eel traps but I was so excited it was almost just a blur. His pots were set in all the most productive haunts on the Taunton River north of the Brightman Street Bridge. They were marked with small dull brown or black cork buoys, not the jugs and big wooden blocks that would draw unwanted attention. Although I seldom noticed them before whenever he shifted the outboard into neutral they always came up on the starboard side where he would snag the line with his gaff and pull the line towards me. Right from the very first one I could feel the life through those cords as the eels began to swim aggressively, pushing against the thick galvanized wire in a last ditch effort at escape. For me it was like opening up Christmas presents. Each pot held a surprise. Some were packed with eels while others only had a few. The non productive pots were stacked up on the bow and we set doubles in the areas of the heaviest concentrations. The two bushel bags of horseshoe crabs that were cut up into bait sized portions wreaked a foul odor from a few days of exposure to the sun and I had all I could do to keep upwind and try not to up-chuck my breakfast. We put a load of eels into his eel crates and all was going smoothly until we hauled our last set in what was known as Marchand's Cove, a location on the Somerset shore of the Taunton River where the owner of the Fall River café of the same name built a fancy home on the shore.

It was a very busy location frequented by commercial shell fisherman and boys like me trolling spinners and sea worms for schoolie stripers. The first pot I hauled there was very light and when it came to the surface all hell broke loose. The genial man in the stern turned beet red and cursed "those bleeping night pirates" then he went into a litany of what was going to happen to the man who tampered with his pots. It only went downhill from there. All four pots in the cove had been pulled and were tossed back empty with the covers open. We knew from firsthand experience that there were a few night pirates from the Warren and Bristol areas that shellfished in these coves after dark. This area of the river had been closed to shell fishing for years but the productive mud bottom was loaded with quahogs that translated into greenbacks for anyone willing to risk capture and a fine. One of the pirates who I'd seen flying up the river in total darkness in his high speed skiff could usually be found working his bull rake in the aforementioned location. One night Paul Lincourt and I were almost run down when we breached the cove while trolling with his quiet Evinrude Fastwin Four. The pirate must have thought that we were law enforcement and closing in so he fired up his engine and damn near ran us down.

After hauling the last of those burglarized pots we headed back into the yacht club basin and transferred our catch to the floating cars Albert kept his eels in. He usually waited until he had a good haul before he drove to Federal Hill in Providence where he always got the best prices from the Italian merchants who coveted his product. The eel fisherman was generous to this young mate, yet he was not the same man I set sail with. Old Pete told me that Albert went to the bar that day, tossed down a few shots of brandy to calm him then went directly to the commercial shellfish dock and issued a challenge and a warning. The word spread that he would be sending a double charge of buckshot at anyone he suspected of tampering with his gear and few men doubted that he would be reluctant to make good his threat.

Over the next few years I mated for him on several occasions and never once hauled another pot that had been tampered with. Alongside the long gaff with the blunt tuna hook that Albert used to snare his marker buoys was a worn green canvas case carrying a 12-gauge side by side loaded with triple ought buckshot. In all the years I knew him I never heard of his discharging that firearm but I learned a great deal about respecting someone else's property, especially on still dark nights when no one else was watching.

THE AUTHOR WRESTLES A 48 POUND STRIPER HE TEMPED WITH A LIVE EEL IN THE MIDDLE OF AN UNSETTELED SPRING MORNING. CONTRARY TO POPULAR OPINON EELS ARE NOT JUST A DEADLY NIGHTTIME FAVORITE.

CHAPTER VI

AFFLICTIONS OF A LONGSHORE FISHERMAN

BACK IN 1972 THE HOOCHIE TROLL WAS CONSIDERED ONE OF THE HOTTEST LURES ON THE MARKET. THE AUTHORS DECKMATE ARTIE GAFFS A STRIPER FROM THE DECK OF CHARLEY'S 22 FOOT HYDRASTEP CENTER CONSOLE. CHARLEY WOULD LOVE TO HAVE THAT BOAT AND A BOX FULL OF HOOCHIES BACK.

I HATE STRIPERS

LOBSTERMEN ARE NOT STRIPER ADVOCATES

"I hate stripers! The net fishermen ought to kill every damn one of them they snare in the fish traps, regardless of size!" Those words loudly articulated in a waterfront restaurant that catered to fishermen caused ears to perk up and eyes to focus on the boisterous redhead at the end of the bar. After a week of screeching winds this was the first day we had been able to venture outside the breakwater and despite roiled water I found a few hungry bass that jumped all over my tubes as though they had not eaten in days. The outspoken lobsterman related that he had been pulling pots on a nearshore ledge and over the past year almost every short lobster he tossed overboard while stripers were in residence were promptly chased down and inhaled by a bass. It was obvious that he was upset about the lack of legal lobsters in his traps but the stripers eating the shorts he was releasing was what really pushed him over the edge. I knew the redhead from seeing him on the water and at the restaurant and I pretty much knew where he set his colorful red, white and orange marker buoys on the various structure. I'd caught stripers on just about every piece of habitat in that area and some locations were much more productive than others. Because I eviscerate all of the bass I keep I'd found lobsters and crabs in their stomach but that was information I had no intention of sharing with the agitated redhead.

While I was in no hurry, or financially able, to buy him another beer I was very interested in the location of that particular reef and if one more brew might elicit a more detailed disclosure of the location I was ready to dig deep. I ordered him a Narry and waited for the information to pour forth. The lobsterman wasn't exaggerating the situation, in fact it was probably much worse than he ever imagined. The previous year I met another young lobsterman who claimed that stripers were "following" his boat to get a free meal of the short lobsters he was discarding. That same skipper took to keeping his shorts in a separate container until he made a high speed run to another string of pots then halfway there he would release the shorts all together. While there might have been a tad of exaggeration it was obvious that the fisherman was dead serious about his plight. Although it took more than my beer, the redhead was pretty well lubricated by the time he slid off the bar stool and headed for his boat so I followed him on the way to my boat which was in one of the same rickety slips behind the restaurant. From what I could see he hadn't made much of a catch that morning and I was surprised that he had not even secured the lobster claws before he went into the bar. While he didn't provide a great deal of information I was able to determine the general location from which most of complaints originated.

It was an area I fished but only on a cursory basis because I had never caught a large fish at that location which was usually picketed by strings (trawls) of lobster pots. It was a deep water ravine between two large boulders and with pots all around it was very difficult to make a clean pass. The next time I fished it I drifted over the deep slot with a live eel on which I pinched a half ounce rubber core sinker on the upper part of the leader. I glided through the gully without incident, but as soon as I lifted my rod to retrieve the snake there was a jarring strike that nearly caught me off guard. My reliable Penn Squidder was in the disengaged mode an option that made those rugged reels such dependable workhorses, so all it took was a smidgen of thumb pressure to prevent an overrun before I engaged it and set the hook. At the bite of steel the fish took off into the maze of pot buoys but I had no intention of losing this fish. I followed and worked my way through the first three markers before I came to the fourth which was now bouncing up and down under the pressure from the bass. I was using stiff but rugged 30-pound line at the time, so I shoved the rod in a holder and hand lined the mono up to the pot up to the top lead line to where my mono was hung up on the splice between the leadline and the bottom floating poly. Once free of the encumbrance the fish took off for the next ledge but she had used up most of her energy on the pot warp and I was able to bring her to gaff without further incident. At that time my electronics consisted of a state of the art Danforth compass and a Heath Kit flasher unit which only provided bottom depth and a barely visible blip for the occasional fish that moved beneath the narrow beam. In trolling mode, particularly where lobster pots are present, it is much more difficult to precisely place your lures and baits where you want them which is why I prefer the more precise drift with bait to get my offering down into the strike zone.

In a perfect world there wouldn't be any lobster pots or gill nets set on striper holding structure, but in an arena where everyone is competing for a piece of the pie the traps are just another part of the overall equation. During my seasons of fishing from Jamestown to Westport I have come to interact and relate with most of the lobstermen and commercial fishermen working those same waters. The same kids that were tending nearshore pot strings with balky outboards that I towed back to the harbor are now running bigger offshore diesel powered lobster boats and it's nice to know there is someone out there I can count on if I run into trouble. Many of those same men share valuable information about bait and fish activity away from my current area of concentration. When I began striper fishing in the ocean in my own boat I had nothing but the aforementioned compass and a wrist watch which was considered adequate for navigation and that was when I became interested in lobster pots and their placement. Lobsters as well as stripers are seldom found over plain vanilla bottom and after years of studying the ocean with my two feet planted on the rocks I began to appreciate the humps and heaves produced by coastal swells. Almost every one of those boulders or spikes had at one time or another had a lobster pot on or around them and from that point on I used those colorful buoys to direct me to structure.

According to my friend Bob Pond and the numerous marine biologists he worked with over the decades, they determined that stripers are what they eat. At one time they were feeding in the upper and mid water levels with menhaden, herring, mullet and mackerel providing them with a varied yet healthy diet. When those fat and oily sources of protein became scarce or unavailable they moved down in the water column and began feeding at a lower level along the bottom where the fare was much less beneficial for their overall physical condition. It was sometime around the late 1980's and early 90's when I began to find an inordinate number of lobsters and crabs in their stomachs At one point my wife counted 13 juvenile lobsters and two choggies in the belly of a 26-pound bass I caught on one of my tubes fished just off the bottom in 22-feet of water. I can't begin to count the number of stripers I have eviscerated, but in the very early stages of my experience those fish were fat and usually full. There were nights at Cuttyhunk in the 1960's when the bottom of my fish box was covered with heavy brown excretions from the anal vents of big fat fish. Friends and clients were worried that those emissions might cost them pounds and contest points and in some very rare instances a few of those husky 49-pounders may have missed the 50-pound mark by a few ounces. One of those stripers, a 49-12 by actual tally on the Clarks Cove fish market scale would have been well over the 50 pound mark if the 15-ounce vent discharge my mate Andy collected in a paper plate from the bottom of the fish box then weighed on that same scale had remained inside his fish. Today I seldom if ever see any such expulsions on the bottom of my large white Igloo coolers which is one more indication that many of these fish are undernourished and some may actually be starving. I have not seen the red headed lobsterman in decades and I doubt his loathing for stripers has abated, but as far as lobsters and pot buoys are concerned I have learned to live with them and I believe I'm a much better fisherman because of that recognition.

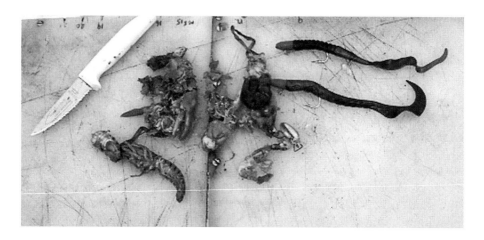

STRIPERS ARE SURVIVORS AND WILL EAT JUST ABOUT ANYTHING THAT DOES NOT ATTEMPT TO EAT THEM FIRST. OVER THE DECADES STRIPERS HAVE MOVED CLOSER TOWARDS THE BOTTOM TO SECURE THEIR NOURISHMENT AND IT IS NOT AT ALL UNUSUAL TO FIND NUMEROUS LOBSTERS, UP TO LEGAL SIZED SPECIMENS, AS WELL AS ALL TYPES OF CRABS IN THEIR STOMACHES. THE AUTHOR CAUGHT ONE STRIPER THAT HAD OVER A DOZEN LOBSTERS IN ITS GULLET.

CONFESSIONS OF A TEMPERATE FISHERMAN

SOBER FISHERMEN SEE MUCH MORE CLEARLY

The last place a man, at least this fisherman, wants to engage in a conversation with a stranger is in the men's room of a sports bar. The door swung open but before it closed the interloper came alongside and put his hand on my shoulder. "That's a hell of a nice catch of stripers you got there." My first instinct was to reach into my right pocket and dispense a burst of incapacitating Crimson Trace. It was barely past noon yet that giant of a man had obviously got a running head start on Happy Hour somewhere else because he reeked of stale beer and fish gurry. In a state between anger and uncertainty I asked him how the hell he knew I had been fishing. "We saw you get out of the truck and walk inside so we figured if a fisherman was eating lunch here that was good enough for us." Suddenly realizing the indiscretion he had committed he quickly withdrew his hand from my shoulder and proffered an awkward apology. I was so aggravated and embarrassed that I stormed out of the rest room without saying another word.   My bride knew something was awry when I returned to the booth but as I was attempting to explain the situation that same man walked out of the head and came over to our table. Before he could utter what I now realize was intended to be a more sincere apology I blurted out "what the hell do you want now?"

He turned beet red and walked away causing my wife to accuse me of hostility toward a stranger. Hell no; he violated my privacy by opening up the cooler to look at my catch, then he accosts me in the men's room and now I'm to blame? Give me a break! Why is it that the player who retaliates to a foul is always the one to get caught and assessed the penalty? What women do not seem to understand is that the unwritten rules of the men's room are, we don't look, we don't talk, and we never, ever touch anything. That was the first and, I hope the last time for such bizarre encounters. Over the course of a lifetime of fishing I've frequented numerous waterside eateries and watering holes and in the process I've had my share of adventures and misadventures. The aforementioned incident with the obnoxious intruder was not the only such recollection. Back when long neck Narrys were selling for $.35 cents at the Fo'cs'le there was another rest room incident that still brings a smile to my face. After a long and exhausting night of fishing I was nursing my then somewhat tepid beer when nature called. The old Fo'cs'le wasn't your rock-um sock-um, blaring music bar but on weekends the city folks would drive down to Sakonnet to hob knob with the fishermen. Friday nights could become a bit problematic as late into the evening we fishermen began returning to the harbor, icing down our catch then washing down the boat before seeking some frosty libation and a bit of sustenance around the Fo'cs'le bar. Unfortunately most of the stools were occupied so the returning fishermen would lean against the wall waiting for someone to leave so we could rest our weary sea legs.

The trouble started when someone hit the rest room and returned to find their stool occupied by some fisherman usually much bigger and meaner than them. That night my stool was flanked by two of the burly, hard working trap fishermen of my acquaintance, who hauled the nets for Carl Wilcox, manually lifted the catch up in huge dip nets then boxed and iced it for market. I wasn't gone a minute before I heard a ruckus and returned to find my friends standing over the prone body of a pretty big guy who had walked up and attempted to take my seat. The guy slid in, pushed my beer and the pack of Dual Filter Tarrytons aside but never quite managed to plant his cheeks on the stool. The barmaid told me that it was over in a flash right after the interloper told Jack to mind his own freeping business. My friend Anthony responded with a well placed elbow that took all the fight out of the bully who had watched two other men, much larger than me, leave their seats before he chose to appropriate mine. What appeared to be an easy mark turned into a choice that certainly ruined his weekend. While it is has never been my intention to paint all fishermen as enthusiastic combatants the truth is that most of the hard working watermen I knew were not given to making long speeches or idle threats.

On another busy Friday summer night I finished securing the boat and locking my catch in the trap house ice locker before I walked through the swinging doors at the top of the long cement staircase. The Fo'cs'le bar was packed and people were standing three deep so I walked over to the men's room to wash my hands before I waded into the throng to place my order for a burger and fries. I was summarizing a fairly successful night and staring down into the sink when I heard a very angry feminine voice up tight to my ear demand, "What the hell are you doing in here?" I looked up to see a lovely young, but very confused woman, three sheets to the wind, who obviously thought I had invaded the privacy of the ladies room. As I recall there were three or four stalls in that men's room and after years of intoxicated abuse only one with a functioning door. The lady (?) was growing angrier by the moment and demanded to know what the hell happened to the doors while repeatedly insisting for me to get the hell out of there. Just then this old gent walked in and greeted the lady in a very courteous manner before asking her if she was dispensing hand towels. Even in her addled state of mind she realized she had stumbled into the men's room and bolted out the door screaming as she went. I watched the mortified female loudly pleading with her two female companions to hastily leave the establishment.

While no one was strutting around with a six gun or a Billy Bat strapped on their waist there was a code of old western justice in place during those precarious years. The fishermen I knew and associated with were basically a tolerant group who lived and let live but God help the person who crossed the line. You never boarded another man's boat without permission and you never, ever opened his fish box or cooler unless you were looking for a broken nose or a trip to the emergency room. Under the influence of alcohol I've watched some normally rational people do some pretty stupid things. As I look back on those formative years in those waterfront watering holes I have come to realize that one of the benefits of seldom being able to afford more than a single brew permitted me to sit on the sidelines and appreciate the show.

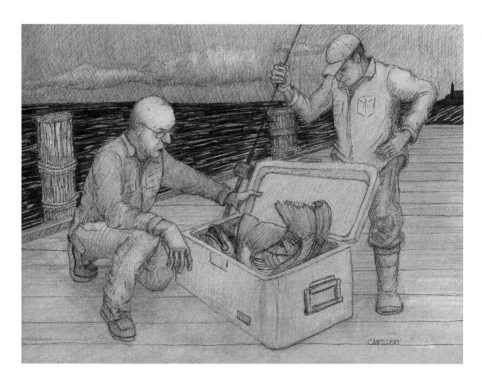

WE KNOW THE WET PAINT SIGN IS THERE FOR OUR PROTECTION BUT WE CAN'T RESIST TESTING IT JUST TO BE SURE. DON'T MAKE THE SAME MISTAKE BY CLIMBING ABOARD A BOAT OR PICKUP TRUCK AND OPENING UP SOMEONE'S COOLER. YOU WOULDN'T WANT SOMEONE WALKING INTO YOUR HOUSE AND OPENING UP YOUR REFRIGERATOR; WOULD YOU?

THREE BEER CHARLEY

DRINK ONE, SPILL ONE AND GIVE ONE AWAY

Three beer Charley was the nickname the affable barmaid tagged me with. I'd been visiting that harbor side landmark since I was a youngster, but it was only a few years prior to the aforementioned designation that I was old enough to sit at the bar and order the trendy drink of the day; a tall frosty Narragansett. From my days of helping serve tables at the boat house clam boils to savoring a win at a sporting event I became aware that food and drink were usually the chosen manner of celebration for most of the fishermen in my circles. At that time 35 cents bought you a beer and for the same price a jumbo order of the best fries in all of New England. The barmaid knew all the regulars and was on a first name basis with all the commercial fishermen in the area and we got along just fine after she told me she would prefer it if I refrained from calling her "mam."After one of my numerous solo night trips I returned to the harbor and iced down 188 pounds of stripers at the A. T. Parascandola commercial dock then walked over to the bar to celebrate my success. It was a slow weekday night with most of the stools vacant so I picked a quiet spot away from the dining room entrance and ordered the Narry. Despite the fact that I had a decent payday coming (at least by my standards at the time) I only had a dollar in change and was undecided about the order of fries I was agonizing over. I finally choose to splurge which would leave me with thirty cents, a quarter of that would go to the waitress.

I was hungry; starving actually, and when a cheeseburger and plate of fries came out of the kitchen for another customer I was tempted to take advantage of the credit extended to familiar customers but wisely I declined. Back then I didn't need willpower because my wallet usually dictated my diet. As usual I was nursing my beer when the cheerful crew of the Xiphias Gladius pushed through the swinging doors and entered the bar. I looked up to see Captain Dave Brayton whose first words were, "drinks all around." The sword fisherman wasn't in her slip when I returned after dark and I wondered if they were lying over off Nomans to get a head start on a second day of fishing. It was a festive crowd in the Fo'cs'le that night. Captain Dave walked over to me and extended his hand. "Are those your fish in the ice house," he inquired, "looks like we both had a good trip?" Dave was a wealthy man who could have been managing any one of his families flourishing companies but after playing the part of the good son (to please his family) when they finally realized his heart was never in business and they gave in. He finally began to do what he was born to do and that was to hunt swordfish. That was back during an era when there was a viable sword fishery off the New England coast and although there were several first-rate harpooners in nearby Westport and New Bedford, I believe Dave Brayton was the best.

Captain Brayton never had a problem enlisting a crew and it was usually difficult getting a spot aboard his 32 foot Brownell. On many an early Sakonnet morning I could be found wrapped in damp foul weather gear while trying to catch a few hours sleep before heading out to catch a morning tide. The startling eruption of his GMC 871 High Output diesel was followed by uneven pulsing that transitioned to a smooth and steady drone. That was my Sakonnet Point wakeup call. After I wiped the sleep from my eyes I watched the crew loading provisions while the skipper inspected the harpoons, kegs and baskets of line that had been a component of the demise of many a huge broad bill. The handsome Brownell only cruised at about 12 knots so a very early start put them on the fishing grounds south of Nomans a few hours after sunrise when the aggressive billfish came to the surface to take advantage of the warmth of the sun. Captain Brayton had taken a liking to this poor boy from the city and was one of the few Yankees to befriend an outsider that were seldom accepted in that tight knit seaside community. After noticing my homemade bamboo creation with a wickedly sharp tuna hook wired to the end he bought me my first commercially made gaff but never took credit for it. One morning I arrived in the dark and it was not until I later reached for my gaff that I noticed the shiny Pompanette gaff alongside it. Later that day one of his regular crew said Brayton had purchased the gaff at a New Bedford marine supply store and instructed him to put it aboard my boat.

On the aforementioned night with the fries and single Narry I soon found myself with three beers in front of me. The kindly waitress came by and with a swipe of her bar rag wiped the condensation around my station and reminded me that the moniker Three Beer Charley was for "drinking one, spilling one and giving one away." She pointed to a down on his luck lobsterman out of business because of a blown engine sitting in the opposite corner who could use a drink so I pushed the sweating bottle towards her as she left with a smile but not before assuring her I was not about to spill the free libation anytime soon. I was broke back then but if no one was around to remind me of that life was pretty damn good for this struggling fisherman. That celebration would carry on well into the night but this boy had to work the next morning. As I was about to leave Captain Dave came over to me and reported that they had stuck five fish that day from a 100 pound pup to a 487 pound dressed weight gladiator that made several violent runs at the skiff they used to haul back the kegs and harpoon lines. I always wondered why there was a big thick sheet of aluminum diamond plate on the bottom of those haul back skiffs until the skipper showed me a photo of a swordfish bill stuck in the hull of a hauled out New Bedford boat. I later heard that one of the boats that I had sailed on was hauling back a sword when it charged the skiff and planted it's bill firmly into the center of the skiff right up through the seat the rower had been sitting on prior to the charge. Brayton patted me on the low back which elicited a wince. He smiled and inquired if I was still hurting from my most recent swordfish trip.

Two weeks prior Brayton had a full crew so I reluctantly signed on to fish with another swordfish skipper who could seldom fill a crew because of his less than stellar reputation. We left Sakonnet Point at 4:30 AM into the teeth of a building southwesterly wind. One of the older deck hands questioned the wisdom of such a trip under those conditions but was assured by the desperate to catch a fish skipper that "it will be much calmer offshore." Those were famous last words. As soon as we came abreast of Nomans Island I was elected to climb up into the crow's nest to spot fins, but with all the white water breaking against the beam of that rolling hull my task was more on a par with a suicide mission. A few more punishing miles toward the Dump I spotted the bow wake of Captain Brayton's seakindly hull coming toward us as they were heading back home. The first mate gave us the thumbs down sign for the deteriorating weather but our skipper kept on going. There were times when we rolled so violently that I felt I could stick my foot out and hit the water as the wide metal band of the crow's nest with only marline whipping around the sharp metal edging cut and battered my body as I hung on for dear life. After Captain Bligh finally acknowledged it was too rough to fish it was much too dangerous for me to attempt coming down from my perch so I hung on and was punished with every breaker we hit on the thirty five mile steam back to Sakonnet.

When we reached the harbor one of the mates climbed the mast, slipped a line under my shoulders and the crew helped me down to the deck. I could not stand on my own and my upper torso was black and blue from my chest to the base of my spine. That was a trip from hell I will never forget. I suspect that many anglers are seeking their fifteen minutes of fame and I soon received my own only under somewhat dubious circumstances. When was the last time a good looking waitress or a hot chick sitting on a barstool asked you to lift up your shirt? I thought so. Over the next two weeks I can't recall how many times I was asked to lift my shirt but it was not to show off my six pack; it was to get a peek at a disgusting mess of black and blue skin. One of the barmaids even asked to touch it and when she pressed it hurt but I bit my tongue and sucked it up. That year Captain Brayton harpooned so many swords, some of them in excess of 500 pounds that I lost count while the manic skipper of the swordfish slave ship never stuck a single fish although he missed so many he could seldom field a group that was hoping for a crew share of the catch. Two days after my three beer night I settled up for my catch and received the princely sum of 45 cents a pound for my bass in the whole which included head, tail and entrails while Captain Brayton received 95 cents for his thoroughly cleaned and dressed out catch. I gratefully accepted my compensation, reached down to stuff my wallet back in my pants and rubbed the still very tender portion of my lower rib cage and decided I had made the appropriate career choice.

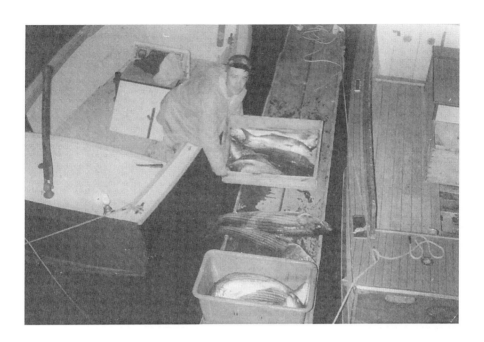

THREE BEER CHARLEY OFFLOADING A SOLO 1960'S NIGHTIME CATCH OF STRIPERS THAT WAS HEADED TO MARKET. THE LITTLE FULL KEEL INBOARD BASS BOAT WAS IDEAL FOR FISHING IN CLOSE TO THE GNARLY SHORELINE.

LIGHTING UP

A FISHING CELEBRATION

Rain hammered down upon the river causing the surface to explode and bubble as thunder rolled and lightning cracked overhead. Our belated attempt to beat the storm was futile yet it wasn't the first nor would it be the last time that greed got us in trouble. We were trolling the power lines along the Mt Hope Bay shoreline when we first sensed the wind shift and felt the cool breeze on our cheeks from out of the west. The sky was darkening as thick gray clouds began to form along the horizon, a warning that was our signal to get out of there or get caught in a powerful afternoon thunder squall. Fifteen minutes before the aforementioned shift; the tide had changed and the stripers had turned on so we decided to make a few more passes along the edge of the submerged boulders that formed a rip along the point. The fast moving storm was bearing down upon us but as we prepared to leave both lines came tight with school sized stripers protesting the bite of the sharp tandem hooks on the Cape Cod spinner rigs. By the time the fish were subdued and slipped into the bulging burlap sack the first big drops of rain caught up with us. The old gent was rowing for all he was worth but he couldn't outrun the storm and in less than a minute we were being stung by tiny shards of hail and soaked to the bone by the deluge. I looked up and watched as the skipper defied gravity.

You would have been hard pressed to find this waterman without a pipe clenched between his teeth and that turbulent afternoon was no exception. With the rain threatening to extinguish the smoldering ash in the bowl the greybeard turned his pipe upside down and continued rowing at a frantic pace. I stared and waited for the hot tobacco to fall into his lap but it never did. For years I'd watched him mix and blend his pipe tobacco on the day-old sports section of his newspaper. He'd arrive with three tins of his favorite brands; usually Bugler, Sir Walter Raleigh and an aromatic mixture then carefully pile them on the sheet of newspaper. When he was ready he moved the different mounds of tobacco closer and carefully blended them into one large heap before reaching into his back pocket for his flask of Mr. Boston's Old Rocking Chair sipping whiskey. Taking a swallow to sample its flavor and to determine its potency he smiled then cautiously dispensed several drops of the rich golden liquid onto the heap before rolling the tobacco in his hands. Even for a youngster who had just begun to acquire an appreciation for cigarettes I knew I was witnessing a labor of love. When he was finished stuffing his blend into three separate wrinkled leather pouches he gathered the particles left behind and packed them into the hot bowl of one of his favorite corncobs.

Waste not want not was much more than a slogan; it was a way of life. At that time about half of the members of the boat club smoked cigarettes and the balance smoked pipes with a fair number of them alternating between the two. There was also a substantial cigar smoking faction who favored a variety of shapes including the long and fashionable panatela. This transpired during an era long before tobacco was relegated to the sinful practice it has become today. Back in the "good old days" tobacco was a form of relaxation and for the sportsmen, particularly, for fishermen, it was a celebratory ritual. The reality is that I can't recall a single angler or hunter, or the rare futuristic woman who lit up in anger or frustration. Although cigarettes, many of them hand rolled with Bugler tobacco, were the choice of the day it was the assortment of pipes and the various aromatic mixes that caught my favor. Pipes were as diverse as the men who smoked them and many reflected their social and economic status. Although there were numerous types of briar with large round bowls and curved stems, and the rare and expensive meerschaum lined bowls, most of the blue collar vets smoked inexpensive corn cob pipes that were purchased for as little as a quarter or a premium grade for $ .29 cents. I was advised that unlike the more expensive wooden briars that required breaking in the cobs were smooth and sweet smoking right from the first light up and as one particularly frugal fisherman noted, it didn't break your heart when you dropped one overboard.

Those were the days when a White Owl cigar cost a nickel during the era when a Red Sox player hit a home run the announcer would shout out "give that man a White Owl." While I was enamored with the aroma of lusty pipe tobacco I could not say the same for cigars, particularly some of those dark twisted specimens. A few grizzled old salts smoked (more precisely bit, chewed and drooled) the nasty cheroots. One particularly disagreeable character smoked the crooks and sported a cigar stained beard that did not win him any friends even among those hard core wharf rats who might wear the same shirts and pants for up to a week or more. My dad smoked a few Old Gold cigarettes every day but he was far from a habitual smoker. He would light up after breakfast, lunch and dinner and perhaps enjoy another smoke before bedtime. Before I began "borrowing" a few to smoke in secret while fishing under the shadow of the Brightman Street Bridge; a pack usually lasted him almost a week. Fascinated with pipes and their aromatic blends I graduated to a corn cob of my own purchased in the village pharmacy for a hard won quarter but this escapade was short lived. Pipes were harder to conceal and carrying around a metal tin or foil pack of tobacco would have exposed my habit so I sold the pipe to another rascal and was happy to be rid of it. Few of us take full advantage of the five senses but I was fortunate to have developed all of my own, especially my sense of smell. There were rare days when the prevailing southwesterly wind was just right permitting me to stand on the top step of the Weetamoe Yacht Club and sniff the air to detect the aroma of pipe tobacco wafting up from the porch. Chief Petty Officer Pete's medley of Captain Black and rye whisky could be sniffed out and his presence confirmed.

Today all that remains of my boyhood sanctuary on the Fall River shore of the Taunton River are the black stumps of rotting pilings yet I can close my eyes and look back. I can see Artie the clam digger leaning back in his rocking chair and firing up his pipe after a few hours of extracting delicious steamers from the unforgiving rocks along the shoreline or Jimmy sitting on the bench relaxing with a pipe after rowing four miles to haul his string of eel pots. There are precious few pipe smokers left however my sense of smell allows me to identify them in public places where the aroma of tobacco smoldering in their pipes brings back fond boyhood memories. Perhaps that's why we were taken aback a few years ago when visiting a Virginia restaurant on a cold February afternoon. That was when the hostess presented the choice of a smoking or non-smoking section, a question that transported us back to the days of ash trays on counters and booths of the local eateries. We were reminded that we were traveling in the tobacco rich country of Maryland, the Carolina's and Virginia where smoking was still a viable inclination.

I haven't smoked since February 12, 1969 when I crushed and discarded the remainder of a pack of Dual Filter Tarrytons that cost me $ 35 cents. Although I am not at all offended by cigarette smoke I prefer sitting around the fireplace at the Addieville Hunt Club in northern Rhode Island where fellow hunters might be celebrating with full bodied red wines, single malt scotch with fine cigars and meerschaum pipes filling the air with the aroma of premium blended tobacco. It's a far cry from the twenty five cent corn cobs and fifteen cent Old Tap, Narry or Dawson ales yet they serve the same purpose. It reminds me that the past can still connect with the future on many levels and that my memories of an era long gone will be treasured and shared with my children and grandchildren.

SALTWATER SPORTSMAN EDITOR FRANK WOOLNER LIGHTS UP DURING A CONVERSATION WITH HALL OF FAME ANNOUNCER CURT GOWDY ON A CAPE COD BEACH AS THEY DISCUSS THE MERITS OF A CLASSIC STAN GIBBS PLUG. IN THE SPORTING WORLD TOBACCO HAS LONG BEEN A MEANS OF CELEBRATION AND RELAXATION.

BURNING THE CANDLE AT BOTH ENDS

EVERYONE NEEDS TO REST BUT THE AUTHOR WAS TOO BUSY TO SLEEP

The first thirty minutes are always the most difficult, particularly for a type "A" personality like me. I've been at this fishing game a long time but the night before a trip never fails to excite me and forestall any semblance of restful sleep; the kicker is if I ever lose that desire and anticipation I believe I will quit fishing and seek out another form of more passive entertainment. I usually awake at least 20 minutes before the alarm goes off and stumble from the bedroom to the bathroom. A few splashes of chilly water startle me into a state of semi-awareness as I head to the kitchen and because the local DD doesn't open until 5:00 AM I make yet another futile attempt to brew a palatable cup of coffee. If Charlie Cinto is on his way down from Plymouth I can count on a giant Dunkin Donut decaf to be handed over as soon as his Jeep comes to a halt in the driveway. It's typically around 4:00 AM and Casey, our Mahoney setter is all excited because the person she loves almost as much as her master and mistress is at the door. That two year old has known Charlie since she was eight weeks old and carries on like a silly girl until she can climb up my fishing partners back and lick him into submission. The tow vehicle is hooked up to the boat and the forward cooler is full of ice. Charlie is finally able to flee the adoring female and runs around the back of the house to dip a dozen or so big eels from my backyard holding tank. Cinto is sometimes in bed by 8:30 PM and even when he's not fishing he is up by 3:30 walking to his workshop to put the finishing touches on another batch of his deadly plugs and bucktail lures.

On this morning we are heading to Sakonnet Point to launch at the cratered boat ramp in Rhode Island where it always seems to be low tide. The cement log ramp is in such disrepair that not a day goes by that even four wheel drive vehicles get stuck in the sand or between the twisted and broken cement logs. Our destination is Newport where the day before I ran a client's boat out of Quonset Point and found some large bass between Seal Rock Ledge and Lands End while fishing my tube and worm outfits. Those fish were encountered at exactly 8:45 AM and if they are still in the area they should be there one hour after on the same tide, but my plan was to backtrack and try to establish where they were holed up before we ran into them. We are ready to move out but I can't find my keys and after 15 minutes of exasperation I remove my wife's spare key from her ring and now a stressed out fisherman leaves almost a half hour after the appointed departure time. We arrive at Sakonnet and on my way around the vehicle to raise the motor and remove the tie down straps I spy my keys stuck in the back window lock where I left them the night before as I put a new pair of leather winch gloves in the rear window rack.

This was not starting out to be the day I thought it would be and with my legs still aching from seven long hours on a rough deck the day before and very little sleep last night the tension was building. A short steam across the Sakonnet River as the sun begins to rise in the rear view mirror and we stop just off at Lands End to rig the live eel rods while Cinto grabs two ice induced snakes out of his eel carrier and places them on the rough toweling. A sharp Daiichi 7/0 bleeding hook is inserted in the snakes and we are ready to begin casting. Did I mention that the muffin that I grilled in the toaster oven fell off the console onto the wet deck and before I discovered it my breakfast was a mess of soaked and mushy cockpit garbage? It was hot and beginning to build into a gorgeous weather day; not the conditions I prefer when I'm hunting stripers. By 8:30 AM it was 87 degrees without so much as a breeze but thanks to the seductiveness of live eels we had two fish in the 30-pound class in the box with two more fish in the same weight class released at the boat. We were looking for just one of the jumbo stripers I saw following a hooked bass to the boat the day before and I was certain we would run into one of them in this area. We were persistent but unsuccessful. Over the next three hours we cast and probed and finally drifted the deeper water but there were no 40-pound bass in the cards for us that day. I was so focused on our mission I didn't have a single thing to eat and nothing to drink and the hot sun was taking its toll. Along about noon I began to feel lightheaded and my legs were cramping up. I sat down on the foredeck and put my head between my knees. I realized I was in trouble.

Cinto, who is, what some might describe as a camel, had not a single drop to drink or a bite to eat was still up in the bow casting away. I asked him to get me a bottle of water from the cooler and that was when he told me I looked like hell. I told him to move us offshore and away from the washes while I tried to get my bearings. My mother was fond of accusing me of burning the candle at both ends and my bride had taken up that mantra early in our marriage when I was pulling all nighters and driving to work daily with less than three hours sleep. Thinking back I recalled that something similar had happened to me many years before while I was making a presentation at the Mass Maritime Academy where I passed out twice and was rushed to Tobey Memorial Hospital. Four days of tests determined that I had been exhausted, dehydrated and my potassium levels had been dangerously low. I never cared for water and did not drink it unless I couldn't get my hands around a coffee, soda or occasionally a beer. Water is life's liquid but I treated it like it was poison and it caught up with me. Those painful leg cramps and muscle spasms I suffered at night were not just the result of six or eight hours on a hard deck they were the result of dehydration. Cinto found an old power bar in my duffel and after drinking the water and eating the bar I was able to stand and get us back to the harbor. We managed to get the boat on the trailer but I knew I was far from being out of the woods so I drove the rig to the first fire station I came across on Main Road in Tiverton where two medics took my vitals and found my blood pressure to be high and my blood sugar to be low and after listening to my history they suggested I allow them to take me to the hospital. I was still in denial so I declined and continued on home.

Later that evening after plenty of water and a good meal I cleaned and packaged the three fish but I didn't feel all that much better. I drove up to the Swansea ambulance building where they took my vitals and suggested I might benefit from a visit to the emergency room. A ride in a hurry up wagon while lying on a gurney with an IV stuck in my arm is not my favorite mode of transportation. An overnight stay at the hospital resulted in a battery of tests and a visit from my attending physician in the morning. He scheduled me for a noontime release after suggesting that I consider abandoning the rigors of pre-dawn awakenings and all day pursuits which were taking a toll on my body and health. I told him that quitting my lifelong vocation was not an option. Just last week I was trying to guide a new friend to his first large bass and I got carried away. We had a total of nine legal and sub-legal stripers up to 35 inches but I just had to keep going to find him a jumbo to prove what a good skipper I am. The night before I had watched the Bruins game until the wee hours and I had been on deck for six hours. I was tired and thirsty when I remembered the water and crackers in the cooler. It's not enough to carry the food and drink-you have to consume the damn stuff! You might forgive me my shortcomings because in all my scribbling I have never suggested I was an intelligent angler. Two bottles of water and a package of crackers later I was refreshed but cutting the quest short and heading back to the harbor. My bride suggests that if I finally admit I'm no longer 29 years old I might just survive to fish another season.

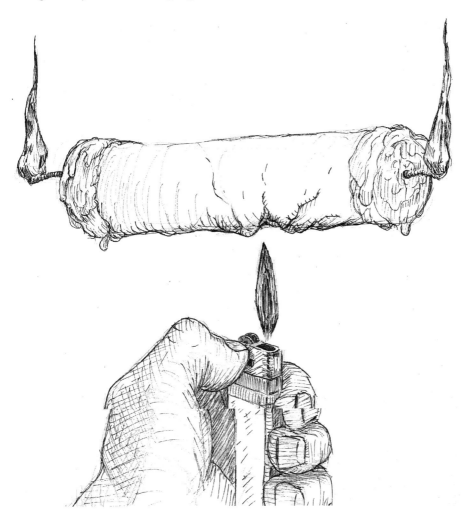

BURNING THE CANDLE FROM BOTH ENDS IS A LOSING PROPOSITION

BRAGGING IN BROAD DAYLIGHT

SOME FISHERMAN WOULD RATHER BOAST THAN FISH

We were trapped. Our plan was to make a hit and run shopping trip to the bait shop to pick up a spool of line, a few dozen worms, and some frozen squid but not before we drove around the block to see if Andy's car was anywhere in sight. Andy was a braggart and a legend in his own mind; a man who would stoop to anything to get ahead and improve his angling image. Russ and I had been trapped by him in the past and it was difficult to get away, but at that time we were into a significant run of big stripers and were doing our best to keep that under wraps. We normally sold our catch in Fall River at Drape's fish market but their prices were seldom as high as those in New Bedford. Andy had a spy who worked on the loading dock that would inform him of all the catches and the names of the fishermen. That was when Andy went to work setting up his surveillance of Jesse's house just over the Tiverton line. Jessie was a fish monger who purchased seafood from the Sakonnet Trap Company where he was allowed to pick through the catches and come away with the best selection, included in that collection was access to the select squid for bait and table. We had a standard order for two pounds a night whether we fished or not and if we didn't show up he froze it and we picked it up on our next visit. Andy was well aware of this and was known to set up ambush to follow the angler or anglers who were scoring big fish at the time.

I had just pulled out my wallet to pay for the aforementioned purchases when Andy surprised us with his hardy greeting and a big grin on his pock mocked face. With no place to run I clenched my teeth and made the best of it. "You guys are on a hot streak; what are you going to do with all the money that Drape's has been paying you?" I told him the news of our success was greatly exaggerated but he pulled an ace from his sleeve and declared that one of our fellow members had told him that Russ and I had entered 40-pounders in that weeks Schaeffer contest. There was nowhere to hide. He scolded us about not sharing information with our friends, which for the record he never was, and suggested it could be very beneficial to us if he joined us. He always had more money than any of the local fishermen because he had a very good job working for his father in law and his wife was known to have won a sizable inheritance from an aunt who passed away during the last year. He tried to wine and dine us because while we were on a bit of a hot streak he had not brought a single sizable striper to the scales in the past two weeks. He was wasting his time.

One afternoon my mother was on her way home after shopping in the P&M Market when he approached her and asked if she would reason with me. He explained that he had always been a friend of my dad and if we shared our spot with him it would be a good way of saying thank you. Andy wasn't one to give up easily and tried working all the angles. Mom wasted no time in calling me to detail her encounter. In no uncertain terms she warned "he has been a lazy man all his life and you and Russ searched long and hard to find your spot-don't tell him anything." During the hot sticky nights of urban summer the residents of Fall River's North End would congregate on the deck of the old Brightman Street Bridge for what my father was fond of referring to as the Village air conditioner. From the elderly to toddlers who found it too hot to sleep in their humid apartments they flocked to the bridge for the taste of a summer breeze off Mt Hope Bay. I can recall steamy July nights when benches, kitchen chairs and rockers were lined up on the south side of the span as residents took in the fresh air off the water. I was reluctant to divulge the following story but in all honesty I feel compelled to. On one of the aforementioned nights I returned from the refreshing cool breezes of the ocean off Newport to the Bridge Diner where the resident short order cook, Dick Branco, mixed me up a cold coffee frappe. I was celebrating the catch of three large bass, one in the mid 30-pound class and the payment that would bring me the following morning. Branco was a devil of a prankster and he concocted a scheme.

Among all the non-fishing residents, Andy the braggart, was fishing along the draw bridge at mid span and had two school bass which he had paraded into the diner to the dismay of two elderly ladies taking a late meal before Branco tossed him out. The cook finally persuaded me to unload my biggest fish along with my rod and get in the vehicle of a willing co-conspirator who would drop me off at the far end of the bridge. My assignment was to offload the fish and rod out of sight on the Somerset side then drag the fish across the entire span where Branco would be waiting with water and ice to wash down my catch. I

157

was dropped off around the corner where no one could see me and had not moved 20 feet onto the bridge when two young men fishing along the rail let out a whoop when they saw the big bass I was dragging. From then on it was complete pandemonium. Andy was still fishing on the rail when he ran towards the commotion. He saw the fish, which dwarfed his schoolies and began howling that my fish did not come from that river but somewhere along the ocean. His admonition fell on deaf ears and although I was tempted I did not utter a single word all the way across to the diner parking lot where the devilish Branco was bent over in laughter. Andy had lost his title of High Hook on the bridge and in his humiliation did not follow us. It was a dirty trick but it earned me a toasted Danish and a brimming ice cold coffee milk.

Andy was not a poor fisherman but he was not a talented one either. Every now and then he would catch what one of my mentors would refer to as a suicidal striper and parade it around town. It was rumored that he once bought fish from a Newport wholesaler to weigh in at Fall River to enter into our contest. He got away with the first half but when he went to sell his catch at Drapes to recover some of his money Frank the buyer turned him away because the fish had already begun to spoil. We never showed Andy where we were catching those fish and despite his dogged following he never tailed us there. He was just one of those men who were never content to work hard and allow things to happen; he was always trying to shape his image usually to no avail. As a boy one of my favorite caricatures from Field and Stream Magazine was of the old professorial fishermen dressed in the most expensive streamside clothing and equipped with the latest tackle fishing on the same stream as the farmer's son. The kid was armed with a simple cane pole and bobber, hoisting a stringer full of fish. The old man with his empty creel wore a scowl as he reached into his wallet for cash to buy a few fish from the kid. Oh happy days!

CAPTAIN ROLAND COULOMBE NAVIGATES THE STEEP GRANITE STEPS ON THE BRIGHTMAN STREET BRIDGE THAT SPANNED THE TAUNTON RIVER. THE TAUNTON HAD A POPULATION OF OVERWINTER STRIPERS AND WAS THE BASIS FOR THE AUTHORS FIRST STORY FOR SALTWATER SPORTSMAN IN 1964

CHAPTER VII CLOSURE

THANKSGIVING BEANS AND FRANKS

TWO FRIENDS CELEBRATE A HOLIDAY IN THE OLD FASHIONED WAY

The green canvas tarp was missing and all that was left of our lean-to was the crude frame fabricated of branches tied together with discarded pieces of tarred handline. Clarkson's boat yard decided the tarp had outlived its useful existence but back then Link and I were the original recyclers. We had this vision of a camp in the wilderness where two self sufficient scouts could survive by living off the land, however, the farmlands and forested areas of the adjacent suburb were the extreme limits of our frontier travels. One of the carpenters at Clarkson's boat house removed the tattered canvas that was protecting the frame of an unfinished boat and tossed it in a heap near their junk pile so I inquired about its fate and was informed that it was being heaved. Up to that point we had been using an old wool army blanket to cover our camp along the shore of the Taunton River but after 15 minutes of rain it not only leaked, but the weight of the wool and water threatened to crush the frail bows that supported our makeshift cover. The green canvas, like many of the tools and equipment that had been discarded by the Newport Navy yard eventually found its way to the boat house via local veterans that were employed there after WWII. The canvas had seen better days with the edges torn and frayed but we managed to cut out a center section that was in pretty good condition. We rolled the heavy tarp up like a rug then tied it with twine in order to facilitate transporting it to the secret camp across the river.

By the time we lugged it up to the top of the stairs we realized it was much too heavy for us to carry through the village, across the bridge and into the woods so I borrowed a wagon from one of the kids and we somehow managed to make it over the bridge and across the busy thoroughfare of US Route 6. We normally took a short cut directly off the bridge and followed the shoreline until we were under the thick cluster of cedar and fir that populated the side of the hill but encumbered by the wagon we walked along the highway then took the farmers access lane down to the top of the hill where we rolled and pulled the tarp close to camp. We were exhausted when we finished but it was worth the effort as the tarp provided protection from rain and hardly moved at all in the stiff afternoon breeze. At the time we were naïve enough to think that our camp, secreted in the center of the heavy cover, was in virgin undiscovered territory, perhaps a place once serving as a refuge for native Indians or early settlers but not a location where someone was likely to stumble into it. The theft of our camps roof shattered our sense of seclusion and safety as we looked upon the bones of the frame. The wool army blanket that served as a ground cloth was still neatly rolled up at the head of the frame so we were certain it wasn't kids that had raided our sanctuary.

There was no clear path into the camp and employing a technique I had either read about in an outdoor magazine or observed in a western movie we never walked (crawled was a more apt description of our form of entry) into the center of the cover from the same direction so as to avoid leaving a recognizable pathway We finally decided it must have been the hunter we occasionally ran into on weekends. He ran a brace of beagles and hunted rabbits and the occasional pheasant in the heavy cover along the side hill and he never responded to our polite entreaties about his hounds or success so it took quite a while before we once again felt secure in our makeshift camp. We had carefully dug a large square pit, about the size of two twin beds and used the sod that was removed to form a wall around the base. We dug a trench to direct the water around the sides and away from the inside where we carefully wove a thick bed of pine and balsam boughs that we spread our blanket over. At the entrance, at least as close to it as we dared, we dug a fire pit and lined it with rocks that we carried up from the beach. We never cut a live tree or branch picking up more than enough driftwood and deadfalls to provide us with warm fires for hours on end. There were times when the wind was from the north and northeast which would cause smoke to blow inside our cover and mom would always comment on how I smelled like a burnt Christmas tree. While we believed our activities were clandestine our hideout was located less than a few hundred yards from the busy four lane bridge and only the width of the river separated us from prying eyes on the urban Fall River shore.

One afternoon I walked into the Weetamoe boat house to see if the caretaker wanted anything from the diner when I ran into an old salt that spent his days on the back porch or warming his arthritic bones by the heat of the woodstove. He smiled when he greeted me and told me that yesterday afternoon he saw thick smoke coming from a clump of trees halfway up the hill on the opposite shore of the river. I looked at him and was about to deny that I had anything to do with that when he reached into his P-Coat and pulled out a well-worn pocket telescope. In his most serious tone he warned that "You'd best use dry wood for the next fire or the Indian raiding party that hunts along the far shore will invade your camp and lift your scalp." So much for the sanctity of our secret spot! Despite the loss of the tarp and the spy on the opposite shore that camp was the place where Link and I celebrated some great adventures. Being pioneers of sorts we believed we could catch, cook and eat just about anything edible however some of our efforts at cooking were awful and downright dangerous such as the time the can of Van Camps pork and beans exploded and we were fortunate to only get plastered with beans rather than shards from the metal can. We soon learned we could cook beans in the can if we made several holes in the top to allow the juices and pressure to escape.

One of the most memorable nights we ever shared there was a meal on the Wednesday before Thanksgiving. Both of us had bow and arrows fashioned from green branches with $.15 cent blunt point arrows purchased from the General Store in the neighborhood. We hunted the briars in the hedgerows near our camp and jumped several rabbits which we usually missed by wide margins. Earlier in the day Link purchased four hot dogs from the nearby meat market and I requisitioned a large can of pork and beans from my mother's grocery closet. By the heat of a driftwood fire we watched a chilly crimson sunset while roasting hot dogs and slurping steaming canned beans. If someone had suggested that I had to dine on beans and franks on the eve of Thanksgiving I'd protest vehemently yet that early evening pre-Thanksgiving meal at our camp was gratifying in more ways than just satisfying our appetites. Our conversation that evening revolved around our plans for the future. Link worked part time at his father's blacksmith shop on Saturdays so he knew what he didn't want to do when he grew up but he wasn't yet decided on any one particular line of future employment. My deep and abiding affection for the woods and waters and my admiration of the local game warden influenced me to select a career in outdoor law enforcement. At the time I was convinced that law enforcement would be the ideal way to earn a living while being close to the places I loved, however that was a course I never pursued. Thanks to the benevolent editor who bought my very first story and encouraged me to pursue a vocation as a writer, that nudge transitioned into guiding and lecturing which became the foundation for a most rewarding life. On your next Thanksgiving when you are gathered with friends and family feasting on turkey and ham think about those less privileged, perhaps those who might consider themselves fortunate if they are eating beans and franks, so if it is at all within your means consider sharing your good fortune with others less fortunate.

A YOUNG BOY AND HIS DOG SIT BY AN ABANDONED HOMESTEAD ALONG THE RIVER AND DREAM OF WHAT IT MUST HAVE BEEN LIKE TO LIVE IN THE DAYS OF THE EARLY PIONEERS WHEN THEY FIRST SETTLED IN OUR AREA.

THE CHRISTMAS GAMBLE

THE GREYBEARDS WERE THE MOST UNLIKELY SANTAS

They really weren't big enough to be called snowflakes but they were the first white specs of the season and that's what made them so significant. It had been a few years since we'd experienced a white Christmas so the snowfall, however light, caused every child who was captivated by the spirit of that special holiday to take the weather as a good omen. With snow falling that close to Christmas even a usually cranky English teacher permitted her students to move to the windows and watch the snow cloak the grimy urban neighborhood in a blanket of white. I'd been desperate for ways to make some Christmas money but with the yacht club all but deserted with the exception of the caretaker and a few of the disabled vets, running errands was out of the question. That didn't mean I didn't do favors for them, I most certainly did but I declined compensation with the exception of the occasional hot chocolate or slice of pie. From what I could determine the old timers were not in much better financial circumstances. That was the year of an abundant run of tautog that lasted well past Thanksgiving weekend when everyone was cheerful and some were even pretty flush. My trips to the diner were frequent and financially lucrative and it was one of the few times in my early years I had actually been able to put aside a few dollars toward Christmas.

That was before two of the woman that mom babysat for lost their jobs. It was a terrible blow for everyone and while the mothers could collect some form of unemployment compensation there were no such benefits for mom. By the end of the second week I heard my mother confiding to my aunt that her meager Christmas savings were going toward food and rent with nothing left for me and my siblings in the way of gifts. In our family it was a single, well thought out gift of some form of clothing and very little in the form of toys under the Christmas tree. I believe my Christmas stash was at $ 3.45 when I decided to buy two pounds of hamburger so mom could make one of her signature meatloaves. Along with that I added two bags of Nestles chocolate chips, a bag of walnuts and a five pound bag of Gold Medal flour, the items from the list which had been attached to the refrigerator for almost two weeks. Mom wanted to do some holiday baking but was just buying the most basic of staples while trying to create room in her budget to insure us the resources to buy a Christmas turkey.

It was a cold and windy period from Thanksgiving to the third week of December and the coal fire in the boat house stove had been supplemented with driftwood we picked up along the shoreline. That month was especially hard on the old time bachelors who got by on small VA pensions and meager social security. I knew just how bad it was when one day I walked into the club and found Jessie salvaging tobacco from the stubs of cigarettes he had saved after he smoked them down to lip singing butts. Camels, Chesterfields, Old Golds and Lucky Strike didn't have filters back then and many of the vets rolled their own smokes in of the trendy Bugler cigarette devices. Those men weren't much on fancy food or accoutrements but there were few situations that came between their tobacco and beer. The Enterprise Brewing Company was a local producer of beer less than three blocks from the boat house and those members fortunate to be employed there would carry home their daily ration of one quart of beer in an insulated jug. Many of those tubs were drained in the kitchen of the boathouse with the aroma of pipe and cigarette tobacco filling the air. About ten days before Christmas I walked into the locker room with an armful of driftwood and was welcomed by the cadre of bachelors who were sitting around a dying fire. With a few pieces of dry kindling and the addition of the salt infused driftwood the stove took on a holiday glow as the men discussed their particular economic predicament. A pooling of their total disposable resources came in at just under ten dollars and that was when they decided to take a gamble. Freddy was a whiz at cribbage and could memorize the discards from up to three games back so it was decided that the grey beards would bankroll him to sit in an uptown card game that was held in various saloons on Friday nights to avoid the scrutiny of the local constabulary. This venture was not without risk because some of the characters in those clandestine games were on the wrong side of the law and it was common knowledge that some of the so called "raids" on those games were not executed by the police. While Freddy was a numbers whiz he was a passive small framed man with a pronounced limp so big Al went along as his bodyguard.

I offered to pray for them but the caretaker suggested that God might not look favorably on gambling as a Christian exercise. Not to be dissuaded I added them to my nightly prayers and bright and early on the Saturday morning I arrived at the top of the shoreline steps to see smoke billowing from the chimney. No one had an automobile back then so it was difficult to determine who was in residence but I took the stairs two and a time and was greeted by wide smiles as I burst in the door. I never found out just how much money Freddy won that night but if the crisp two dollar bill they handed me was any indication he must have hit the jackpot. The caretaker peeled a five dollar bill from an unfamiliar wad, a rarity at a time when some men carried small leather change purses to prevent money from falling through the holes in their well worn pockets, along with a list of groceries he would need for our noontime meal. It was a feast fit for royalty and I went home with plenty of leftovers to share with my family. Mom skimped and saved that December and with tears in her eyes she confided in me that we would have our turkey but there would be little left for a few toys for my siblings and perhaps a shirt and some socks for me. Although I was mature for my age mom's candor was distressing.

My deportment was evident when I visited the club so I confided in the old timers who collectively improved my outlook. As I was leaving the club the caretaker told me to keep my chin up because the Christmas season was the time when dreams came true. That was an unusual statement from a very pragmatic man but I chalked it up to the season and left to do some shopping. That two dollar bill had been burning a hole in my pocket but along with the lone dollar I had saved I headed for the downtown section. I avoided walking by the sporting goods store and headed for the Fanny Farmer candy store. Mom loved ribbon candy and at thirty nine cents a pound it was a buy. I went through ten sheets of scrap paper trying to budget my funds but it always came out the same; I didn't have enough money. I left the upscale candy store that sold me two boxes of ribbon candy and two of their signature chocolate mint bars all gift boxed for mom before I left for the Five and Ten to purchase two large bags of assorted candy for my brother and sister who would not appreciate the pricy upscale brand our mom loved. Their toy department was loaded with a large assortment of affordable games and I purchased one for each of them. That same store had a lunch counter with ice cold Richardson root beer and the best hamburgers and hot dogs in the city and after avoiding it on two passes I gave in and treated myself to a pre-Christmas lunch.

Bus fare was a nickel back then but I had a light load and decided to pocket the coin and jog the four miles back to the neighborhood. I hid my stash at my aunt's house where she promised to wrap them for me. I headed for the club where the old timers were sipping outlaw brandy distilled in the basement of a nearby three family house. There were bags and bags of what appeared to be groceries and dry goods on the counter and as soon as I walked in I was hustled away to the locker room and sent on an errand. When I returned there was no sign of the bags, just an empty bushel basket on the counter. We enjoyed our refreshments and exchanged holiday greetings before I departed. Late the next afternoon it began to snow and it was coming down hard during our Christmas Eve walk to my aunt's apartment. I was the first one up on Christmas morning and looking out the window to see how much snow had fallen I noticed a set of tracks leading up to our front porch. I opened the door and was surprised to find an overflowing bushel basket loaded with candy, food and gifts. Once mom and the kids peeled off the upper layer I spotted a full box of hooks then a spool of Ashaway linen line. Next a pair of rubber gloves, two pairs of Wigwam wool boot socks and two hanks of 27 pound test marline line. At the very bottom was the wool plaid shirt from the window of Pratt's Sporting Goods I had been wishing for. Everyone was so excited while I was awash with joy, sadness and extreme gratitude.

Looking out the window through teary eyes I saw the tracks in the new fallen snow leading away from our porch in the direction of the boat house that indicated that Santa had well worn size 10 boots with a decided limp and drag marks on the left leg. As soon as I dressed I hurried to join those grand old timers that saved this country, made it the best place to live and were an adopted family that shared tough love with a boy looking for instruction and direction. I will cherish those men and the memories we shared until the day I die. Merry Christmas!

GOD BLESS THE OLD TIMERS FROM THE WEETAMOE YACHT CLUB. THEY WERE MENTORS AND PROTECTORS OF A BOY LOOKING FOR DIRECTION AND A MARINE EDUCATION AND THEY PROVIDED BOTH IN GENEROUS QUANTITY.

BURIED TREASURE

DON'T PERMIT YOUR OLD TACKLE TO BE BURIED WITH YOU

It was a well worn Penn Sea Boy; the most basic and inexpensive of the revolving spool reels but it was finally a reel of my own. Everett was one of the many wounded veterans who returned from the Great War with a serious wound, in his case to his right hand and when he handed me the reel he tended an apology along with it. That old reel with the stained linen line had been in his cellar for years and every time he looked at it he believed he would someday be able to use it. Rather than improve; the limitations to the hand he sacrificed to save our country, became more severe. Earlier that week he was part of a group of old timers who were putting together an order for me to fetch from the Bridge Diner. His usual order was a black coffee and a plain donut but while he was scratching around in his weathered change purse, it was obviously short on coins. He just smiled and said "just a coffee" and put the exact change in my hand. As the errand boy carrying orders to the diner I was granted certain favors and one of them was my choice of a donut whenever the waitress with the winning smile was on duty. On that day I chose a plain donut and decided to serve Everett last so no one would notice that he was the recipient of my charity. He walked over to the porch railing where I was trying to catch an eel and winked at me and on his way out. In the course of our conversation he told me to meet him at his apartment after supper that evening.

Having no idea what he had in mind I was concerned that I may have overstepped the boundaries of civility and offended a very proud veteran. My concern was unfounded. I was greeted in the friendliest manner and directed to the basement where he showed me what he had left in fishing tackle. One of those items was the aforementioned scarred Penn Sea Boy single action reel, some tarred line, sinkers and a weathered box of Kirby tautog hooks. That was when the apology was delivered. The old timer explained that he had watched me struggle with the tangles in the old tarred line spool I had been fishing with and said he often thought about giving me the remnants of his tackle, but for some reason he never got around to it. He confessed that it was my decision to give him my five cent donut that caused him to realize that it would be much better to put that gear to good use rather than have a relative toss it out after, as he referred to it, "checked out" and have it go to waste. Along with that tackle was a slightly used spool of linen fishing line that was a gift of his sister, who formerly worked at Cordage Park in Plymouth, Mass, where they wound the line on wooden spools, a relic from a bygone era. In hindsight, I wish I had saved the line rather than used it to cast for eels and white perch along the shores of the Taunton River. To this day I'm still looking for another spool of Cordage Park line and one from the Assinippi line works of that same era.

In the ensuing years as he watched me fishing from the first pier of the Brightman Street Bridge or casting from the gas float at the yacht club he smiled and was thankful that something he had no intention of using, was being enjoyed by someone and he admitted that it gave him great deal of satisfaction. Many years ago the father of a family friend had a considerable amount of money in CD's and savings bonds but he would not part with any of it during his lifetime because his depression mentality would not permit him. He told me they would get the money when he died but the state had other plans and the vast majority of his money paid for a very lengthy and painful stay in a nursing home. That was an example of why people should consider enjoying their good fortune with their families while they are still with them. During my lifetime I have witnessed the treasures and memories of the past being buried with the person that owned them rather than being shared with their family while they could appreciate them. Not just the physical items, although in a few cases there were some articles that went to ground with their owner. Earlier this year a friend showed me a custom hand crafted bamboo fly rod that was the property of his grandfather, who in turn left the rod to his father. The three piece rod was carefully cased in a soft red cloth sock and protected in a metal container, both of which were produced with considerable care and skill. My friend was interested in having the rod he inherited restored so it could be displayed in his home where he could share memories of his father with family and friends. I have no doubt that the rod was expensive, even for that time and today that 80 year old heirloom is more than a fishing rod it is a priceless family heirloom.

A rob builder friend took great pains in restoring the rod to as close to original condition as possible which included travelling to Green Harbor to secure a spool of winding thread that closely matched the original. When I returned the refurbished rod to the owner he made me a gift of some old tackle he found among his late father's possessions. One of those items was a very old Penn Sea Boy reel which at the time of their introduction cost somewhere in the neighborhood of three dollars. Penn made so many of these reels that I have bought them at yard sales for two to three dollars, but the one from that man was special because it was as close to the reel that Everett gave me so many years ago. I have begun to restore that old single action and will put in on display with the other old collectable fishing gear I keep on the shelf on our side porch. If you have old fishing tackle, hunting or camping gear you should think about making a gift of them to a family member or a close friend with a detailed explanation about the item. In the case of a reel that information should include by whom and when it was purchased and how it was used. I am fortunate to own a great deal of new fishing and hunting gear yet I still get a kick out of stepping back in time by casting with and old single action reel which illustrates the skill required of past fishermen to make trouble free distance casts and retrieves. I often wonder how many of the larger specimens of striped bass I have been so fortunate to have brought to gaff that I would have landed if I was handicapped with this primitive tackle. While my contemporaries are always interested in tackle from another era it's the children who are drawn to the shelf where an assortment of reels dating back to 1875 is attracting the dust that my bride takes me to task for. The youngsters, particularly the children of fishing fathers, are bursting with questions about the where, when and who of a particularly curious looking item. Don't bury the treasures of the past with your loved ones. Take the time to inventory those sporting items that may be of personal rather than monetary interest to other family members or friends and make them a gift of it. Old tackle should not be discarded or buried with their owners. These treasures can evoke and perpetuate fond memories of those who are no longer with us.

THE BOY WAS STARING AT THE SILVER JEWEL OF A REEL AS THE OLD TIMER TURNED ITS HANDLE AND DRIFTED BACK TO HAPPIER TIMES. CHARLEY THOUGHT THAT REEL MIGHT ONE DAY BE HIS BUT THAT WAS NOT TO BE. IN HIS TRAVELS HE HAS SEEN VAST STORES OF TACKLE IN DUSTY BASEMENTS, GARAGES AND ATTICS THAT WAS DISCARDED BY FAMILY AFTER THE OWNER PASSED ON. CONSIDER MAKING A GIFT OF AN UNUSED OR UNWANTED GEAR THAT WOULD BRIGHTEN THE LIFE OF SOME DESERVING YOUNGSTER.

EPILOGUE

I would be less than honest if I told you that the striped bass was not my favorite species. From the very first time I watched a handsome striper hand lined and hauled up onto the rocky Taunton River shoreline I was hooked for life. Up until that time I'd been exposed to the winter flounder, white perch and the occasional tautog but that silver striped fish I had learned about from the tales of the old timers conversations pushed me over the edge. Striper fishing had a hook in me in the beginning and I have no doubt it will be there in the end.

With that said I must confess that anyone who fishes exclusively for stripers is missing out on a world of exciting and rewarding angling. Those anglers in New England who limit themselves to stripers can realistically look forward to a season that runs from early May through mid October this means about six months out of our year when we can't bend a rod. I usually begin my season fishing for white perch sometime in early March and top off the early months with tautogs and cod right up through Thanksgiving. That schedule limits my withdrawal time to a mere three or four months, much less than the striper purists who confine themselves exclusively to New England waters. If you have never felt the joy of resistance of a winter flounder reluctant to give up the mud bottom of an April backwater tidal flat or tried to pry a bucktoothed tog from the rocky lairs, wrecks or the rotted pilings they frequent I feel sorry for you. In this day of limited bags and closed seasons adding other available species to your bucket list will extend your season as well as providing you with some delicious eating.